EVERYDAY VIOLENCE

How Women and Men Experience Sexual and Physical Danger

ELIZABETH STANKO

An Imprint of HarperCollins*Publishers*

Elizabeth Stanko is an American criminologist now living in London and lecturing at Brunel University. She is the author of *Intimate Intrusions: Women's Experience of Male Violence* (1985).

Pandora
An Imprint of HarperCollins*Publishers*
77–85 Fulham Palace Road,
Hammersmith, London W6 8JB
1160 Battery Street,
San Francisco, California 94111–1213

First published by Pandora 1990
3 5 7 9 10 8 6 4 2

© Elizabeth Stanko 1990

Elizabeth Stanko asserts the moral right to
be identified as the author of this work

A catalogue record for this book
is available from the British Library

ISBN 0 04 440426 3

Printed in Great Britain by
HarperCollinsManufacturing Glasgow

All rights reserved. No part of this publication may be reproduced, stored in a retrieval system, or transmitted, in any form or by any means, electronic, mechanical, photocopying, recording or otherwise, without the prior permission of the publishers.

CONTENTS

	Acknowledgements	v
	Preface	vii
1	Introduction	1
2	Common Sense, Routine Precaution, and Normal Violence	13
3	Searching for a Safe Place	35
4	On Learning Safety and Danger	51
5	Women, Femininity and Safety	85
6	Men, Masculinity and Safety	109
7	Climates of Unsafety	130
8	Safety and Protection in Modern Society	145
	Notes	155
	Bibliography	161
	Index	165

for Rosa and Tony

ACKNOWLEDGEMENTS

As a feminist, I have focused my endeavours over the past 12 years on how to ease the burden of men's violence within women's everyday lives. Violence, for women, is so common that it often goes unnoticed. This book began back in 1985 when I turned my thoughts to how criminology, as a discipline, explained the phenomenon of the fear of crime and in general neglected the high levels of fear reported by women. In many respects, this is as much a study of gender as it is a critique of criminology.

It has taken me a long time to complete this book. Professional and personal demands took their toll on my ability to think. I changed jobs, countries, had a baby and somehow expected that I would be able to write unencumbered. It is not possible. I have required support and assistance throughout this project. Clark University's faculty development fund seeded the study. My Clark University students allowed me to talk at length about these ideas. In particular, I am grateful to Maria Amador, Sarah Cullen, Martha Dooley, Kathy Karl, Jeff Knudsen, Ray Lemieux, Debbie Mancini, Marla Maritzer, Ray Pifferrer, Leah Rogers, Scott Rubins, Stephanie Schneiderman, and Jessica Sutin, all of whom participated in my seminar on gender and safety. David Shulman and Mark Ballam, as research students, started the preliminary work on men and fear. Diane Hamer and Sandy Munger transcribed many of the interviews with ease and grace.

ACKNOWLEDGEMENTS

Nigel Fielding, Jeff Hearn, Mike Maguire, Tony Jefferson and Paul Rock commented on earlier drafts of the manuscript. I deeply appreciate their time and effort, as men as well as busy academics. I am also thankful to Marty Levine for sharing his thoughts on homophobic violence, and to Liz Kelly for her drive and commitment in demanding a better life for women. Whilst I know I have not answered all their queries, I hope that this book sparks more interest in how we experience crime and danger in our everyday lives. I beg the forgiveness of my academic colleagues who have debated and discussed this issue with me. I do intend to take these musings into the academic world, so bear with me.

I am truly indebted to Dee Dee Glass, whose vision of this book and demand for clarity kept me going when I was so willing to abandon it. Her good humour, unselfish editing, and pressure pushed me through many of my blank moments. Kathy Hobdell also kept me going, and our project exploring men's reactions to violent assault will follow shortly. Philippa Brewster, my editor of eight years, waited patiently for this manuscript. She understood better than I did that having a baby did interrupt even the best organised lives. And many thanks to Debbie Licorish for her calm manner and eye for detail. Finally, may I thank Tony Green for all his support and good humour during the most trying of times, and Rosa, for just being Rosa.

PREFACE, 1995

Many people living in the western world in the mid-1990s seem to feel at more and more risk of personal violence. Politicians wail about the rise of violent crime, legislate against the growing mayhem and promise longer sentences for the menacing criminals on our streets. If we take a look at news headlines in the five years since this book was published, we are faced with a litany of violence. As ever, violence sells papers and gets people to tune into the news. But have we become or are we more aware of the sort of violence which is *most* typical of life in the West? The official and unofficial information we have about crime continues to tell us that the familiar and the familial pose the greatest threat to our personal safety. The situations that have occupied our angst and our viewing times – in the United States, the double murder of Nicole Brown Simpson and Ron Goldman, the rape of Diseree Washington, Lorena Bobbitt's assault, to name but a few – should have led to questions about the nature of 'everyday' violence, that is, violence done to us by our familiars. In Britain the killing of the toddler James Bulger by two 10-year-old boys might have been averted by the 38 adult witnesses who *mistook* the trio for brothers; the implication is that brotherly abuse is somehow tolerated, or somehow not seen. Someone would have intervened if they had known strangers were involved.

Meanwhile our fear of strangers persists. Not that some who walk the streets around us might *not* sometimes bring us serious harm; but this kind of harm has such a disproportionate domination of the headlines, the politicians' legislation and the warnings to our children. I too receive the cryptic notes from my six-year-old daughter's school (at least every few months) warning me about a man who might snatch her or expose himself. I also fear the dangerous, male stranger.

Other facts, though, persist. Violence, while sometimes random, is usually directed – at men by men, at women by men, at the 'other' by mostly men and some women – because of race, religion, accent, lifestyle, sexual orientation, able-bodiedness, in short, hatred or intolerance.

We have responded. Some of us by minimising our time in public space for fear of encountering the random menace; many by purchasing a range of weapons, locks, bolts, alarms, and insurance; parents, by acting as virtual bodyguards for our children; governments, by dispensing crime prevention advice which promotes individual responsibility for keeping crime at bay. But has this reduced our fear? Or contributed to our greater security? Clearly not.

Unless we tackle the collective lessons of our experiences of violence – for both women and men – then we will not be able to promote any comprehensive social policy to promote domestic safety, let alone to reduce or minimise the violence of the street menaces.

Even if we somehow convince individuals to live careful lives, we usually forget that such care is expected where danger often lurks: at home, or in other situations where we trust others not to harm us. This book aims to look behind the headlines and the industry of fear, and to prompt us to think about violence in a more reasoned way.

Elizabeth Stanko
London, April 1995

Chapter one
INTRODUCTION

In late October, 1989, two items appeared in my local paper, *The Worcester Telegram*. One described a recent tragic event which became *the* symbol of senseless urban violence. Carol and Charles Stuart left a Boston, Massachusetts hospital pre-child birth class in the early evening of 21 October. According to Charles Stuart, as they were stopped at a traffic light, a man pulled open the car door and forced him at gunpoint to drive to another part of the city. Carol was then shot and died soon after doctors delivered her baby boy. The child died seventeen days later. Charles sustained gunshot wounds and recovered.

The wake of the shootings churned up the ever-present concern about public safety. Many metropolitan police departments, including my local department, reacted to the killings in Boston by offering the public advice about their safety on the street. Worcester citizens, who live approximately 50 miles from where the shooting took place, were advised by police to take the following precautions:

- It doesn't matter where you live, you have to think there is a possibility of danger when you go somewhere in your car. Keeping aware at all times can make a difference.
- Park in the busiest areas of shopping centres or hospitals because there is less chance a problem will occur.

- Stay in well-lit areas when you bring your car to a stop.
- Plan on your worst expectations as a matter of course. Once you have made the proper plans, you will feel more comfortable and safe, and less likely to face major problems. Overall, concluded the police spokesperson, 'Just stay on your toes.'

The possiblity of confronting random violence frightens us, especially when we hear about the murder of a pregnant woman by a stranger. In this instance, as reported by her husband, the assailant was black, further cementing the racial image of a ruthless criminal as a black man. Identified by Stuart in a police line-up, a 39-year-old suspect was harshly treated by police in custody. The response of the black community in Boston was anger toward a white establishment that treated the death of a white woman as a priority over the number of daily violent deaths of people of colour. Without question, the American media, police and local politicians ranted and raved about pointless violence, gun control and vicious criminals, fuelling racial tension and fear about personal safety for the largely white Boston population.

But the case took a curious twist when Charles Stuart killed himself, jumping from a bridge into Boston harbour early in January 1990. It seems that he had become the prime suspect in the murder of his wife, that he hoped to profit from life insurance policies and that he had shot himself to prove his story. The public horror of random violence, telecast nationwide on *911*, a popular network show narrated by William Shatner, and shown on the breakfast and evening national news programmes the day after the shooting (film-crews just happened to be riding with Boston police that night), is the hidden terror of private violence. Carol Stuart's assailant was her husband, the father of her child. It was too easy to believe that a black stranger could be so cruel – for *he*, rather than a loved one, has become the symbol of urban danger.

INTRODUCTION

A second item in the local paper that late October told of a birthday party held in Brooklyn, New York. At some point during the party, a fight erupted and thirteen people were shot, one critically. The police issued a statement saying that no one who attended the party would talk about what had happened. Some who read this news item may even have smiled wryly at the scene of mayhem. The police did not respond with warnings about attending parties. And very few people admit to a fear of violence that spills from personal disputes.

Danger, many of us believe, arises from the random action of strangers who are, we further assume, usually men of colour. Yet according to most people's experiences, reinforced by the statistics of academic researchers and police alike, danger and violence arise within our interpersonal relationships – spouses, lovers, relatives, friends, acquaintances and co-workers pose the greatest threat to women's and men's personal safety.

I

At some point nearly every day we hear fragments of stories about the latest bank robbery, mugging or murder. Newspaper and television reports deluge us with ever-swelling crime waves. Blame gets laid variously on bad parenting, bad character, bad blood or occasionally on drugs - but almost always on the shadowy stranger, just out of reach. Governments periodically declare war on crime. Yet, somehow, those of us who are meant to feel under constant threat expect to go about our ordinary lives undeterred by the risk of becoming the next victim. Or do we?

Increasingly, few believe that the strong arm of the law will protect them from the harm caused by those bad people. To allay our fears, we are inundated with advice on ways to avoid becoming targets for crooks. This comes not just from the police and other official bodies, but often from the same media who splatter the news with blood-curdling stories. And now, as the task of fighting crime shifts from the police to neighbourhood watch schemes, citizen safety becomes evermore the responsibility of the individual.

In this book, I explore the efforts of most of us to manage danger, both sexual and physical, in everyday life. It presents information from interviews conducted in London, England and the New England area of the United States. Men and women, black, white, Hispanic, Asian, rich and poor, heterosexual and homosexual, speak about their own understanding of personal safety. Housewives, students, professional workers, tradespeople, unemployed or retired, ranging in age from 16 to 72, share their experiences, precautions, worries and fears about personal danger posed by their fellow citizens, some of whom they live with, some of whom they share their neighbourhoods, and others of whom are complete strangers.

II

Research by criminologists over at least 25 years has focused almost entirely on anxieties directly related to violence from strangers. This so-called 'fear of crime' has led to increasing government expenditure on fear-reduction programmes, and to a proliferation of law-enforcement schemes promoting the notion that mass participation in crime prevention makes good sense. Many police forces today have special units whose sole job is to encourage citizens to feel more responsible for their own safety.

One of the recurring concerns of criminologists is that this fear of crime is somewhat unfounded. Perhaps exaggerated by the popular press's fascination with violence, it is believed to be related not to direct experience, but to impressions of danger or to a mistrust of strangers. Lurking outside the home, faceless assailants seem to transform the outdoors and unknown others into targets of suspicion.

Generally speaking, researchers and policy-makers alike characterise the fear of crime as a destructive force, interfering with full participation in everyday life in a civilised society. Many people, for example, avoid certain sections of a city or a neighbourhood, hesitating to frequent shops, theatres, pubs, or sports events because they are anxious about their personal safety. Also, worrying about being attacked or having their homes invaded by burglars causes an exceptional amount of stress for certain groups, especially the elderly and women. These people have had crime-prevention and fear-reduction programmes specially designed for them. Ironically, those who report feeling safest are statistically at highest risk – men. Young men who are single, spend most evenings out and engage in social drinking are, according to surveys, most likely to be victims of crime.[1] While men who reside in higher crime areas do report higher levels of fear, even men who say they worry about violence do so at levels one-third that of women. Risk, some researchers theorise, is a reflection of how often one leaves the safety of one's own home.[2] Actual personal danger, as opposed to perceived personal danger, these researchers further speculate, relates to how an individual exposes him or herself to violence.

III

My approach differs from the traditional studies of criminologists in several ways. First of all, rather than viewing violence as a disruption to the supposedly calm life we lead, I perceive it as an ordinary part of life. This is not to say that I accept violence as good or even natural, simply that modern social conditions make danger a reality. Nor is it to say that most individuals experience violence on a daily basis. Some do. But the majority have learnt to manage violence, some with more success than others. If any of us takes measures to try to guarantee our safety – such as staying alert on the street, resisting arguments with our intimates because their bad tempers might lead to a beating, or avoiding certain public places that make us feel uneasy – we are automatically taking violence into account as a possible occurrence in our lives.

Exploring how individuals negotiate the daily threat and experience of danger is the primary focus of my approach. Abuses of personal safety often happen during routine activities. Handbags are snatched as we do the regular food shop. Wallets are stolen on our journeys to and from work. Physical and sexual assault is most likely to occur during normal social activity, and within seemingly ordinary courtships and marriages. Damage to our houses or cars, which we often feel to be violating, happens while we sleep or are out doing mundane chores.

Having to negotiate danger differentially also affects us. This is as much an exploration of how different types of people experience their lives within seemingly free societies as it is a study of how violence affects us daily. Depending on our social circumstances - on where and how we live, or on who we are - we gather experiences of safety and danger and come to perceive situations as safe or as dangerous through our own accumulated experience. We also come to understand our own effectiveness in assessing likely peril. These variations in individuals' perspectives can be found in the results of crime surveys. They report that those who express the most concern are people of colour, those on low incomes, the elderly and women. Information about attacks on homosexuals, though not collected by crime surveys, points to the fear for personal safety within the lesbian and gay community. Those who have the least privileges, it seems, are also burdened with the additional task of worrying about their own security.

While other criminological works concern themselves only with the potential threat posed by strangers outside the home, I do not assume that the home is safe.[3] The place where people are supposed to find solace from the perils of the outside world should not be presumed to provide a respite from interpersonal violence. For far too many, menace lurks there as well. The prevalence of battering among women's experiences of intimate relationships with men, the growing awareness amongst adult women of potential and actual sexual danger from male intimates, acquaintances and friends, and the memories of adults of physical and sexual abuse during their childhoods shatter the illusion of the safe home.[4] Despite this, risk is still assessed by criminologists as being largely associated with strangers. The myth of the safe home and the continued focus on the dangerous stranger overshadows many people's own knowledge about personal safety.

The portrayal of those paralysed by fear of dangerous strangers seems to be a favourite image of the media and, at times, the police. Law and order enthusiasts speak of those imprisoned inside their homes for fear of attack. Better policing and greater government efforts are demanded to stop crime. Those critical of the government attribute citizen fear of crime to social disadvantage, as well as citing the huddled, anxious populations of 'no-go' areas of the city. One gets the impression that people who are afraid of crime or interpersonal violence are in a constant state of anxiety. No doubt, there is a sizeable minority of individuals who feel that way under certain circumstances. I have spoken to some of them. But the majority of people actually cope with their anxieties on most levels, whatever concerns they may have about personal safety. We shop, work, socialise, care for children and for our homes as full participants in modern life. It is *how* we cope that is of interest here.

IV

Basically what we do is to manage danger. It is a continuing, conscious, although mostly routine, process. Many individuals report elaborate strategies to avoid the risk of violence or possible intrusion of their homes or property. Some say they feel safe while describing in minute detail how they walk down the street monitoring the behaviour of all those around them. Others state that they feel very unsafe, yet they travel about because, they say, the 'usual' precautions are taken. We invest in locks and alarms for our homes and cars. We learn to read the signs of potential danger from many different clues such as the presence or absence of people on the street, the temper or irritability of the person closest to us, the funny feeling in the pit of our stomachs, the nagging doubt that something is wrong, or the recognition that a situation is similar to one where danger occurred in the past.

As we grow older, we continue to learn to read and reread situations and other people both for safety and for possible danger. We monitor our physical surroundings and have a shorthand for reading where potential risk might lie. Dark streets, alleys, deserted buildings, parks, subway cars, and night-times provide us with information which we assess for safety and for danger. There may be places we may visit during the day, for example, but never think of going to at night. And vice versa. Sometimes the threat is located in characteristics of individuals. Many people express anxiety when they come upon a group of teenage males. Women often report concerns about stepping into a lift or an elevator when even, and especially, a lone man is present. Or people of colours' experiences of racial harassment may make them wary of the behaviour of whites. Information is growing about violence motivated by hatred. The calculation of those who are, historically, targets of such hatred must be recognised as a grounded fear of the physical and sexual dangers of power. Recipients of such violence, homosexuals for example, might take additional precautions to avoid situations where they face potential attack. This strategy is more difficult where those who are most likely to be harmed are surrounded by those who have more power. Negotiating danger is in many respects negotiating power.

V

I present here an argument, not an empirical or definitive study about the nature of violence and personal safety. The media, police, government officials and most criminologists agree that public concern about violence, threat and fear

INTRODUCTION

is best focused on the ravages of faceless criminals who make our streets unsafe. The police advise us to become 'streetwise', and to stay alert in public. Politicians promise to increase police expenditures to fight crime.

The current thinking about safety and danger fails to capture what people know and experience as personal violence. Whilst our attention is continuously attuned to that which happens in public places, there is a stony silence, almost a denial of the extent of violence that happens in private, usually between those who already know each other, however slightly. To the extent that it is acknowledged at all, we assume that this private violence is normal. Real violence, that committed by strangers, is abnormal, an affront to public safety.

But women and men learn about safety and danger from all their experiences. Yet, the barriers of shame and embarrassment have silenced thoughts of private violence. And what does get reported has important implications for understanding what it means to be male or female. Violence is assumed to be the domain of men, as perpetrators and as recipients, at least according to criminological knowledge and resulting government policy. Feminist research, though, clearly shows that women's lives are marked by a continuum of male violence.[5] Women, it seems, experience much of men's violence as private violence. The public discussion about women and violence only acknowledges women's fear of attack at the hands of strange men.

While women's concern may now be recognised, at least on the level of male violence in public places, men are assumed to go about everyday life unimpeded, unless, of course, they worry about their wives or children. It is even acceptable for men, it seems, to talk about violence and danger as if they are exciting, and, for some men, actual participation does bring exhilaration. But we have no idea how danger and violence affects men, particularly if they are, according to crime surveys, often the targets of other men's aggression. These experiences are rarely articulated.

The purpose of this book is to explore the dimensions of being a gendered person through an examination of how women and men experience safety and danger. To illustrate my argument, I rely on the words of women and men interviewed between 1985 and 1989. Half of the 51 interviews used for the purposes of this book I conducted myself. The other half were conducted by my students who were enrolled in a seminar exploring gender and safety during the autumn of 1987.[6] I constructed a detailed interview schedule that asked about the kinds of physical and sexual threats each respondent experienced before their 17th birthday, and after. The students used this interview schedule in their own studies. In the interviews I conducted, I found that the flow of the interview improved as time went on. I followed the direction of the discussion, rather than the direction of my interview schedule. People recalled threats, and violent events, not chronologically, but as a series of similar situations. Each interview was transcribed verbatim. I also held a number of group discussions about personal safety during those years. These group discussions became sounding boards for my observations about the patterns of women's and men's understanding of personal safety. They helped confirm my observations or sent me back to muse further on what I was thinking.

I am a trained sociologist, a specialist in criminology and criminal justice. For the part 17 years I have focused my teaching and writing on the victimisation of women. I continue to be amazed by how much of women's lives and the understanding about women and violence is absent from the criminological literature. What feminist researchers have documented over the past 20 years is the continuous thread of violence and intimidation that runs through women's everyday experiences.[7] It comes as no surprise to me that women's fear of crime continues to be so high.

I began to ask women if they could describe the little things they do to make themselves feel safer. I tried this once in a women's studies course and the students cited example after

INTRODUCTION

example for over an hour. I realise that since women are used to taking responsibility silently for their own sexual safety, the everyday precautions they exercise articulate silent oppression, an unspoken expectation of being a woman. Indeed, women's lives are more complicated because of their concerns for personal safety. And the danger, women themselves know, is not always the faceless stranger. But it is the confrontation with the stranger that is the curiously controllable feature of managing danger. A woman might at least choose which street she will walk down, or whether she carries her keys in her hand or in her pocket. She never chooses her family of origin, and rarely chooses intimacy because a partner or friend is known to be dangerous. Yet many women's experiences of danger and violence come from men who, through family or familiar connections, may strike under the cloak of privacy.

While most of those I interviewed assured me they lived relatively uneventful lives, few if any were untouched by violence. One woman, a 63-year-old widow, assured me that she would not have very much to contribute to my study. When the interview was complete, she recalled being fondled by a shop owner when she was 8, feeling physically threatened by her brother as an adult, being attacked as a nurse while working at night in a hospital and being hassled by men for sexual favours after the death of her husband. My sensitivity to the hidden violence in women's lives directed my discussions with women. And because I am a woman myself, I tapped into my own understanding of self-protection and used this knowledge to encourage women to articulate what I knew to be women's 'common sense' about protection.

The men were more difficult, by far, for me to interview. Initially, I could not find an easy way for men to discuss feeling danger and threat. Having men abandon the illusion of invulnerability, one mask of masculinity, was a tall order indeed. I decided to change tactics and interview men who had recently experienced a violent attack. The men talked and they began to reflect about how the attack made them think about personal safety. So I developed a repertoire of men's language about danger and some techniques for encouraging men to think about safety as something they do, not just take for granted. Inevitably, after I presented my thoughts to groups or professional meetings, a few men would quietly reveal threatening events in their lives they had only recalled while I was speaking. Men, too, need to examine their understanding of personal safety, and begin to break their silence about their experiences of violence. I hope that this book stimulates such speculation.

My argument about safety and danger is illustrated by the prose of the men and women interviewed in both the US and UK. I will not present a comparison between the Americans and English people to whom I spoke. No doubt, some of the dimensions of danger and safety differ. The most glaring difference is handgun ownership. The glossy advertisement for Smith and Wesson's *Lady Smith*, the designer women's handgun, would seem curiously crass in the UK. The gun is casually displayed on a side-table, nestled with the leather gloves, mink coat and a fresh rose, as if they all go together naturally.

I begin with women and men describing routines and strategies for safety. These strategies often lead people to search for places where they feel safer or where they can feel comfortable, as if safety is located geographically. The next chapter examines how women and men learn about safety. The lessons of danger and violence arise throughout our lives, and this chapter explores the knowledge of danger we accumulate with age. The following two chapters examine being female and being male, and the relationship of femininity and masculinity with understandings and experiences of sexual and physical danger. Finally, I explore what it means to be a target of violence within an intolerant community, and the experiences of intolerance for the lesbians, gay men and people of colour interviewed.

Chapter two

COMMON SENSE, ROUTINE PRECAUTION & NORMAL VIOLENCE

This chapter is about everyday routines of safety. These are not the habits of paranoid people who find difficulty in coping with the ordinary demands of daily life, but behaviours typical of adults. People develop these routines in order to avoid being constantly preoccupied with security: little rituals which seem to reduce their anxiety about danger. They take these measures in their homes, on the street or at work as safeguards against being attacked.

Some habits do not seem to have any conscious origin, but they are things people say they have always done or were once told to do by someone in authority. Such tips for safety are incorporated into our lives without much question, and we come to consider them as just good common sense. We pass them on to our children in the hope that they, too, will be safer and avoid danger.

If there's an occasional familiar ring to what people say in what follows, it's because many of us do similar things, including having rituals for locking and unlocking doors, choosing routes to and from shopping or work, protecting valuables inside and outside our homes, carrying money, travelling to strange places and assessing the who, what and where of safety. Some of us have habits few know about and we keep it this way for fear others might consider us odd.

One of my quirks, for instance, is having to have a clear shower curtain, so I am always able to see the whole bathroom. Some attribute this to an all-too-careful viewing of the movie *Psycho*, but I know that I feel more comfortable taking a shower when I can watch out for interlopers. Even though I have cats who always insist on opening the bathroom door to keep me company, I cannot overcome my anxiety that it may not be a cat who comes through that door. So to put my mind at rest, I have a clear shower curtain. For me, that curtain is a device for my personal safety. Seems daft?

Over many years, I have heard a wealth of stories like these which may sound a bit crazy to others. One woman, for instance, never uses a hair-drier if she is alone in the house. Another checks her bedroom closet for possible intruders before she can go to sleep. When his girlfriend is out of town, one man sleeps with a hammer beside his bed. He then meticulously explores each room, opening closet doors and checking window locks. Important to each of these rituals is that, once completed, it is possible to feel safer while at home. The thought that others may view the performance of such rites as just a little weird perhaps accounts for the silence that surrounds them. Nevertheless, their potency is not thereby diminished.

You sceptics who are sure that no one you know does such ridiculous things, ask those close to you whether they have routines they use to protect themselves from burglary or assault at home or in the street. Have your friends or relatives recently purchased new locks or alarms for their homes or cars? Do they feel comfortable going out during the day? What about night-time excursions? Listen to the responses, for patterns of concern about personal safety will emerge.

One of the most noticeable is that women report practising a wider variety as well as a higher number of safety rituals than men, in many ways illustrating a greater awareness of their vulnerability to violence. While women are often accused of being overly cautious about safety, those very same accusers might well be the first to blame women for making themselves vulnerable by venturing out to so-called unreasonable places at so-called unreasonable times. This usually means that women must silently juggle their safety and their avoidance strategies with autonomy and independence.

There is, of course, a wide range of differences among women. Those, for example, who live in inner-city areas develop skills involved in reading the street. The skills, as many will already know, include the ability to judge the behaviour of those around you as well as constantly assessing your physical environment for signs of danger. Combinations of strategies vary, depending upon age, race, sexuality, physical ability, experiences, living situation and where in the city their homes are located. Women in middle- and upper-class areas with a high level of home-ownership and a concomitant degree of influence over their environment may see danger quite differently from those living in largely rented or publicly-controlled housing. Few middle- and upper-class women would even think of walking or driving into many of the areas where poor or low-income women live. Women in public housing, often located in areas reputed to have high rates of crime, share the skills of monitoring danger with middle-class women. However, less affluent women's levels of anxiety and stress, and the practice of continuously looking for signs of danger, take a much higher toll on their quality of life. There are, indeed, differences in the levels of perceived and actual safety of 'outside' space depending upon one's economic resources and one's ability to choose where one lives. Nevertheless, whatever their economic circumstances, there are similarities in how women experience violence from men they know.

Although greater precautions are taken by women, both sexes pick up clues about what safeguards to use from their own individual circumstances. As social and economic status affects how we understand possible threats to our safety, the relative security we feel is one aspect of rank and privilege. Those who have low incomes and less control over where they live are the very individuals who mention anxiety more often. Others, who can afford them, will ease their fears by buying more locks and similar gadgets or by moving to a 'safer' neighbourhood.

Do members of any one group say they are actually immune from personal violence? Probably not. But some have more barriers to it than others. Car-owners rarely contemplate the problems of danger on public transport, unless they use it regularly for commuting to work or for leisure. Those who live in 'nice' neighbourhoods expect at least some civility on the street. The able-bodied, and male, assume that they can defend themselves and hardly think they are vulnerable to sexual assault. People who can afford burglar alarms and heavy bolt locks never consider housing with flimsy doors or accessible windows, and certainly would not dream of living without adequate household insurance.

So when people speak about rituals of safety, they are describing both their perceptions of their needs and the extent to which they are able to go about protecting themselves. The economic, social and political contexts in which they live their lives are rarely acknowledged, as these seem to be entirely taken for granted. But they all recognise the old adage: 'I'd rather be safe than sorry.'

STRATEGIES FOR SAFETY

On the Street

> I always have my keys in my hands wherever I go and I have a whistle and I always have my arms free. I always know right where I'm going and I never stop and look at things.

> I've always been aware of someone walking behind me, and groups of youths, black or white. I'd cross over to

COMMON SENSE ROUTINE PRECAUTION & NORMAL VIOLENCE

> the other side of the road. I always took my key out of my bag and put it in my pocket, just in case.
>
> I have a couple of night classes. I'm usually by myself. I don't know. I usually don't think about being attacked or anything like that. I just kinda go. I don't focus on anybody. I just focus on where I'm heading to. I look straight ahead. I don't make eye contact. I usually don't carry too much money. And my clothes I wear to school are usually just jeans and a sweatshirt. I usually don't carry more than 5 dollars with me.*

Especially within an urban area, being 'street smart' means moving purposefully, alert and on-guard, unencumbered, and with the confidence that one could respond to danger quickly if need be. Risk comes from making eye contact, from unwittingly missing the signs of danger. These streetwise rituals, commonly used coming and going from home at night, include varying the routes home; walking on the streetside of the sidewalk or pavement; avoiding dimly-lit areas, bus stops, or train platforms; walking assertively; selecting parking spaces carefully; avoiding certain districts at various times of the evening; never carrying valuables in a handbag; having friends or companions wait outside until one is safely inside one's home. Some people actually carry a limited amount of cash to surrender to muggers if the need should arise.

Certain routines are also treated as necessary in order to be able to leave home, sometimes during the day, but mostly at night. Micki participates in martial arts purposely as a hedge against personal danger, and she consciously monitors her surroundings at night.

> I become more aware [when I am out at night]. I get ready in case something happens. Like if I have to run,

---

* The extracts throughout this book are exact transcriptions. The text that appears in square brackets has been added by me in order to clarify the sense or the context of the response to my questions.

yell, or fight. If I have my hands in my pockets, which I don't do anymore, I take them out. I walk 'bigger' and I try not to have anything on my person that would get in the way, like a loose jacket or something, or books. When I have a backpack, I don't sling it over one shoulder anymore. I put it over both so I can use my arms if I have to. But that sort of happens every day. I don't ever feel completely safe. I feel less safe at night. I don't know why night has these connotations but I guess studies have shown – I don't know if this is true or not, but this is one of my assumptions – that stranger attacks happen between six and midnight or something like that. I can't see as well then. And it's night, and the mystery of scary bushes and stuff like that. It's harder to be familiar with the environment. It's like two different environments almost. So I don't feel quite as safe then. I'm more cautious when I go out at night. It's also a stereotype – night-time is when these things happen, even though they happen all the time. So I'm used to walking real big.

One woman, Maria, uses companions to help her secure her own safety:

> I don't go out at night unless it's with someone. If I'm going out with friends, they will always pick me up at my door. When I come back they'll walk me to my apartment and make sure everything is OK. I always have someone with me, even if it is to walk from my house to the car.

What I find so often in speaking with women is their own recognition of their special vulnerability as women on the street. This awareness is demonstrated in the way they are able to describe, sometimes in minute detail, the routes they take home, using their vehicles, if they have one, as devices to secure their own safety. Cars, for many women and some men, become mobile safety units. Soon after being physically assaulted by strangers while he was walking down the street, Alan remarks: 'I go out at night but only if I can use the car.' Men may be prompted by a specific threatening experience to find additional ways of increasing their personal safety. But for most women, it is a matter of everyday routine. Sylvia, employed in what she feels is a 'high crime area', explains how she uses her car for her coffee and lunch breaks.

> [Where I work] probably has as high a crime rate as any other part of [my city]. Maybe a little more. I'm not sure. Lots of drug dealers. You can watch that on the corner if you care to. My work is on the intersection of where the drug stuff goes down. But I don't walk by those corners. If I want to go up to the diner to get a coffee, I will drive up, even though it's only a couple of blocks. But I don't walk past the people on the corner only because they're all males for the most part. They have been drinking and you know, who needs the aggravation? I mean obviously they're going to feel compelled to say something to me and even if they'd rather not, they have each other to impress. They're going to have to say something to me and I don't want to deal with that. So I will drive. Maybe ten years ago I would have forced the issue and walked, but now I don't look for any added aggravation.

To understand the logic of keeping safe, it is important to appreciate the ability to anticipate the possible 'aggravation' or trouble one may find on the street. Someone who has been menaced recently or has experienced memorable threats in the past, may become acutely aware of possible danger. Or someone may be living through a particularly trying time. The death of a loved one, a divorce or separation, or other life crises may bring on additional feelings of vulnerability. Sylvia assumes she will encounter harassment, at the very least, on her coffee break, if not greater problems from the probability of violence that surrounds drug deals. During the course of her working day, she sees countless others passing by the corner and how they are treated. She rightly places herself amongst the likely targets – why should she be any different?

What feels safe to some may feel unsafe to others. Just as the car can be a security device, it may also be the location of danger. Kathy describes leaving the shelter of her car, not just to get to her home, but anywhere:

> My car is parked in a lot a little bit down, a block away. So I feel a little nervous at night when I go home. I only walk a block but I'm really aware of the block that I walk. [When I go out] I definitely try to park in well lit areas and I try to park close to the place [I'm going]. I'm really conscious about making sure that if I do go out that I park in somewhere safe. I lock my door [when I'm driving].

Approaching the car after an evening out is also recognised as a potential danger trap, as Jane states:

> When I get into the car, I always check the back seat, to make sure that there is no one lurking around. I always have my keys in my hand, so that when I get to the car, I could stick the key into the door. I don't get to the car and then have to start stumbling around my bag for the keys. My keys are in hand already. And I lock the doors right away.

Walking alone at night often gives rise to uneasy feelings in women and some men. But many have no choice but to either walk alone at night or stay indoors. 'I really don't like walking alone at night, anywhere,' states Kathy. Large-scale victimisation surveys, as I have already noted, support the findings that women express more concern than do men. These surveys also show that under 5% of those interviewed state that they never go out at night, because they fear for their personal safety. Among elderly women in inner-city areas, this figure rises to almost one in five, nearly 20%. Yet, most of us say that we do venture out at night.

So when we do walk down the street at night, and in some neighbourhoods even during the day, there are a variety of rules of thumb we adopt for protection. One woman, for instance, regularly visits the fish and chip shop on her way home so that if the need should arise, she can always run in there and feel secure. (She complains that this strategy caused her to gain weight, however!) Lester, an elderly gentleman from Central Massachusetts, copes by restricting his own behaviour:

> I don't walk home after 8 o'clock at night from downtown. The idea of walking home from here at 10 or 11 o'clock at night doesn't appeal to me. That has cut into my life a little bit. Obviously though, in either daytime or night, in the crummy area around my house, I do my best to have eyes in the back of my head and be very alert to who is walking where. I am more firmly resolved not to let myself walk home drunk.

During a group discussion in Massachusetts, Mark describes his ever-changing map of safety:

> When I go to this one section of the city, I'll walk down this side of the road and when I get to this other section, I walk down this side of the road, and when I get to this other section I walk on the other side because there's less houses and less people will be sitting outside on this side than they are on this side. You know, if you really think about it, then you're carrying your keys because they can always be used as a weapon if necessary.

Jane, a resident of New York City, reports:

> You know which streets are bad, and you know which streets the drug dealers are on, and you know which streets the prostitutes are on, and you just stay off those streets. You stay on the streets that there's a lot of people. If you go into the city [Manhattan] enough, you are going to know where the good people are, where the bad people are, where it's crowded, where it's safe to walk, where it's not safe to walk. And if you just know that about the city then you're OK . . . But I feel safer when [my husband] is with me . . .

If we live somewhere we know has frequent, random incidents of crime, we take additional precautions. One man reported that how he walked at night depended upon 'the neighbourhood in which I'm living.' Mike reports:

> Like I lived over on [a notorious street for crime] and I'd go out at night to the drug store to get some cigarettes or a newspaper or stuff like that. Basically my concern was not having too much money in my pockets when I go out. There were some of the men [where I worked] who had gotten jumped. I knew that some people's houses had gotten broken into. But largely it was the money situation which was a real concern, not wanting to lose too much money if I ever got jumped. I wasn't walking faster or being much more cautious or something. I think there was probably a certain amount of fear but not a whole lot.

Mike also said he worried about the possibility of a chance meeting with 'a couple of big guys . . . if I don't know them and I think they tend to be threatening.' The threat here is the threat of physical violence. It is the rare man who mentions the possibility of facing sexual violence, with an exception being the man who finds himself in prison. Both heterosexual and homosexual men aim their precautionary behaviour towards the avoidance and negotiation of physical safety. Margaret, who has lived in her neighbourhood for 27 years, perceives the time of day as a clue to her safety:

> It depends on the time [of the evening]. I think early in the evening I would do it [walk] without too much problem, but probably after 9.00 or so I would be careful. I used to go for walks a lot. It would get dark, and I would take a walk. And now I wouldn't do that.

In a further effort to protect themselves, some people carry objects which can be used for defence, such as lit cigarettes, keys between fingers, knitting needles (one of my own favourites), umbrellas, pens, or personal alarms. Others carry actual weapons. Cynthia reports:

> I have a key chain that has a [small] knife. I keep that in my hands but nobody bothers me but I keep it as a precaution. I look back [while I'm walking] once in a while.

Deborah also mentions weapons spontaneously:

> I found myself the other day walking down the street carrying a penknife in my hand. I knew that if somebody came up to me I wouldn't do anything. I wouldn't even take my hand out of my pocket. I suppose that it did make me feel a bit confident. I still felt a bit silly, walking around with a knife in my pocket. Something I always do is I hold my key. I've got a massive key and I just hold it. Somebody said that if someone comes up to you just stick the key in his eye. Like I wouldn't be able to do that.

Neither of these women quite know what they would do with their weapons, but holding them makes them feel better.

While some people carry objects in order to feel better, others pack weapons because they work, or participate in activities, where violence is part of the scene. One American man who earns his living through various illegal activities admitted to carrying a gun for persuasive protection:

> I quit smoking because it was affecting my ability to physically defend myself. I think the street has gotten a lot worse over the years. It was bad when I was a kid, but it's gotten a lot worse over the years. There are a lot of drugs and stuff like that. I carry a gun, and if that doesn't do it, just my strength [will protect me]. I'm protected. Your safety is up to you. You're only as safe as you and luck will have it sometimes. Sometimes you'll just be at the wrong place at the wrong time.

While this particular man may be philosophical about risk, the possibility of facing violence is part of his livelihood. He does take precautions, as do others who participate in lucrative, criminal enterprises where violence is part of doing business.

What is especially interesting in the US, where many women express concerns about their own safety, is that it is men who are more likely to pack guns and knives.[1] In Britain, too, men more than women carry knives as weapons. Men bear arms to even the odds in any confrontation with other men, while women who have an object in their hands do so to help them feel more confident on the street or as a way to meet male intimidation. It is important to remember that men report that, by and large, they feel relatively safe.

Safety at Work

The risk of attack at work, as well as during the journey there and back, is also of concern to many people. Nurses and other hospital staff, police officers, probation officers, prison officers, school teachers, bus drivers, shop clerks, bank tellers, security personnel, salespeople – they all have contact with those who may be a danger to them. Threat may be a regular part of the job, from bullying school children or troublesome colleagues to potentially violent clients and customers. Or it might come from the occasional stranger either at work or when commuting.

Again, it is women who report taking precautions aimed at both sexual and physical safety, while men speak only of physical safety. Sexual harassment at work – the composite of experiences of sexual degradation from verbal assault to sexual assault – should also be understood as an obstacle to the security of women and some men. One woman whose job was to canvass for a non-profit organisation in rural Massachusetts carried a can of mace (a personal safety device containing a liquid stunning agent) with her. Laura states:

> I carried my mace because I had a job canvassing [membership subscriptions] last summer. You went from door to door all throughout the night, asking people for money. They [the supervisors] dropped you off. You had a really long turf, and they'd meet you at the end. A lot of times there were certain places that were really creepy at night. It was basically country areas and really nice places, you know, because you wanted to get a lot of money. And there were some places. I know one night there was this fog and I couldn't see anything. It was half raining. And some guy told me, 'You shouldn't be walking around late at night,' and I was really feeling weird. I was walking away from his house and was getting the eeriest feelings in the world. I was holding on to it [the mace] for dear life. That happened to me a few times in that job. I was doing it because I was getting a lot of money and I totally believed in the cause.

Robert, an electrician's apprentice in Central Massachusetts, tells of his concern for his safety at work, where the danger comes from colleagues:

I had a situation at work within the last year. I almost got thrown down a flight of stairs by a guy about twice my size but it was strange because it was over something where he was angry over the fact that he was making only 25 cents more an hour than me. I guess he didn't have anyone to take it out on but me. I knew I couldn't take him on. And if no one was going to be on my side I was going to have to do something. A lot of people I work with I don't trust, and doing electrical work, it would be nice if I did. So I just watch my back. If I'm working on something, I'm going to check and double check because, not having trust is like the same as having incompetency. It's like somebody that's not going to turn off a switch when you're going to work on something.

The strategies we devise for safety on the job may include some of the things we already do on the street or at home. One woman, for instance, took her dog with her if she had to work late at night or on weekends. When estate agent Suzy Lamplugh disappeared from her office in West London in 1986, concern about the vulnerability of women at work rose to alarm levels. She went to show a house to a potential male buyer and never returned. Her diary indicated the time, place and name of the client, but there were no other clues about who he might have been. For a long time after her disappearance many women changed the way they interacted with male clients. Some estate agents in London now require all clients to meet the agents in the office first. Some agents will show houses only in pairs. In 1988, when a 14-year-old schoolboy disappeared while delivering newspapers and was later found murdered, two-thirds of the paper delivery children in that rural area left their jobs.

While this kind of acute anxiety rises and falls, perhaps partly due to particular highly-publicised incidents, some people feel acutely vulnerable and alter their work habits permanently. When danger occurs in the ordinary work routine, worry about safety may completely interfere with the ability to do one's job at all. Some leave because they are no longer able to cope with the daily reminder that they could be attacked. Many others have been utterly silenced about their fears for safety because they fear being accused of incompetence.

Each individual must find ways to quell his or her concern regardless of the particular climate of safety. Jill, a Londoner, describes here the daily planning of her return from work as riddled with vigilance:

> If it's the end of a working day and there are a lot of people moving around, then I have this general underlying kind of consciousness that you just have to watch your back a bit, but I don't feel scared at all. But I do consider which route I will take home. I have three routes: I can either go across the park, which I never do at night, under the bridge, which I never do at night, or up the main road, which is the route I'll take in the dark at the end of the working day. Similarly, if I was having to walk home in the dark for some other reason, that's the route I'd take because I consider it the safest.

Kathy reports:

> On a regular basis, I do a couple of things which I have come to do in the last few years. I tend to move my car late at night. My job is 9 to 5, but I certainly don't leave my office at 5. What I do is around 5 when most of the people are leaving the city I will go and get the car and move it to the front of my office. And that I feel is a protection because at 8 o'clock at night, I'm not walking down a dark road by myself.

Some employers recognise the unease of their employees. In Croydon, near London, for instance, local government staff are allowed to park their cars in front of the town hall if they must work at night. This means that those parked in the multi-storey car park across the square often move their cars at around 5 p.m. for their own safety. When I lived in New York and commuted by public transport from Manhattan to the Bronx, I would regularly choose which route to use going home. It depended on how tired I was, whether I had a travelling companion, what I was wearing and how much time I had. These variables were flexible ones which I negotiated day to day. But I also had fixed rules, standard practices which enabled me to make across-the-board decisions about what I needed to do for my own safety. I dressed down as much as possible, covered up any jewellery, kept my handbag clutched close to my body, stayed near to other passengers, selected train cars where there were as many women as possible and the one in which the guard operated the subway doors. I followed these regulations stringently.

Safety at Home

> I just don't have much in the way of fear. One of the things I do, by the way, when I go home in the evening or anytime I go home, I always open the apartment door and look around to make sure there's nobody in there.

While 72-year-old Lester may not be afraid to enter his home, he none the less takes some precautions when he does. The simple procedure of looking around the home is one tactic people use as part of routine behaviour. Others keep televisions and radios on and lights burning when going out at night, or use electronic timers that automatically switch on such appliances when it gets dark. Dogs are trained to bark at intruders, perhaps frightening them away. Thanks to modern technology, people may even purchase a tape recording of a dog barking for their burglar alarm.

Nowadays locks that are highly elaborate, expensive and considered to be the most impregnable are growing in popularity. The majority of people say they regularly lock their doors when going out. Some household insurance companies even specify what kind of security a house must have in order to qualify for coverage. Indeed, firms specialising in domestic security are making bigger profits.

Protecting one's home against thieves is also procuring one's personal safety. Those who are burgled sometimes report feeling intimately violated as well. Others treat it as a hazard of contemporary urban living. No matter what the individual reaction, no one wants to confront an uninvited guest in their own home. Margaret, a 62-year-old woman, widowed and a resident of a small city in Massachusetts, has experienced four burglaries over the past six years.

> I guess I don't feel that it is as safe [as it was when I moved in 27 years ago]. I think it was the kind of thing that if I forgot to lock my door I didn't get frantic about it. Now I go around and check the locks. My windows have the nails through them and I have a whole lighting system set up so lights go on and off all over the place all the time. I have a very expensive light bill.

Gordon, a 23-year-old man, living in a small town in rural Massachusetts, states:

> There's two doors that lead out of the apartment and they both have chains on them and a deadbolt. When I'm in the apartment, I always have the deadbolt on the doors. One door is always locked. That's the door I never use. If you're in the bathroom or you're washing up or you're doing dishes, or something you can't hear if someone's coming in, and then it's too late. If someone comes in . . . Not that I anticipate it, but why risk it? And when I'm home for the evening, the door's always chained. I have a sliding glass door in my living room and even on a day like today when

it's a beautiful day out I wouldn't leave it open even though my living room faces a quad in the [apartment] complex.

Ricardo, a resident of Central Massachusetts, feels that danger may arise without warning and speaks of those safeguards he uses to protect himself and his family:

I'm always expecting the unexpected, you could say, taking caution in everything. I like to take care of the house. I always make sure that the house is secure and also the family. I tell the children never to open the door without asking who it is. When I have to go out for a couple of minutes, I tell them to say I'm in the bathroom, to leave a name and phone number and say I will call them back in five minutes. Never to say they are alone.

People are able to describe the tactics they use to safeguard themselves against intrusion from outsiders. The 1984 US Victimisation Risk Survey, for example, shows that people have taken measures to protect their property in their home. One quarter of the respondents of this survey indicated they had engraved their property so that, in the event of a burglary, their valuables could be identified if recovered. The 1992 British Crime Survey finds that 20% of households in England and Wales keep an eye out for intruders on a more formal basis through neighbourhood watch schemes; US figures show that approximately 7% of US households participate in neighbourhood watch.[2] While the majority do not participate in organised neighbourhood activities to protect against burglary, they do take some measures to deter household crime by installing locks or by making the house look occupied at all times.

Yet, no matter how secure your home may be to intruders, if you live with someone who is violent, either physically or sexually, the potential for danger is locked in with you. The targets of this kind of violence, typically women and children, try all kinds of avoidance tactics. Rachel recalls:

> My dad would beat up my Mom, and me or one of my sisters would call the police if it got really bad. Or if my mom told me to call, and then they would come. I was really scared, for her and for me, because it was really obvious that if he was going to hurt her, he would hurt us too. I was really concerned about her, trying to figure out how to make it safe for her, to do something. It was frustrating because there was nothing really I could do, because he was so much bigger and things like that. I was frustrated and angry.

When you live with your assailant, part of monitoring danger lies in carefully observing the behaviour of the threatening person. Sylvia states:

> I have lived with one partner who came to be unsafe. I don't know when I began to view it as unsafe. I think it took more than a couple of shoves for me to realise that it was becoming increasingly less safe. I finally left when a gun came into the house. I figured it was only a matter of time before that became the next stage in the acceleration.

Just as the home can be the location for unsafety for those living with violence, it may also be seen as a fortress for locking out danger. Linda, who now lives in Central Massachusetts, moved from one city to another after the experience of rape by an intruder. She describes the hardware built into her present home:

> We built this house because I had been raped. We really built it. I think everybody thinks we're crazy. I've got locks, you know. Our doors are really good.

We have grates on the basement windows, that sort of thing. Very small windows at the top. [The house is set up] high enough so that somebody can't look in. I keep the windows locked, lock the door at all times. I'm certain that someone could get in if they really wanted to, but when I look at the other houses around, it would be much harder to break into this one. So I feel apprehensive in general, but somewhat more safe within this house. I'm apprehensive going from here to the car and back . . . which I think is probably more my own psychological reality than actual. Well, I shouldn't say that. It [violence] happens all the time.

Anticipating trouble prompts some to keep their homes as uninviting as possible, reducing the possible attraction of the target. Jill, living in London, describes the logic behind her caution:

I've got lovely ideas for the front of the house, but quite honestly I don't know if it's worth it. And it's not that doing it would actually cost very much money. It would simply be a coat of paint and maybe a couple of pots so we can plant things growing up the wall. It's a dreadful thing to say that you don't actually want to do the front of your house simply because you know you'll get burgled if you do. But I do keep a pretty low profile. I'm particularly cautious about the front door because it's right on the street so it would only take someone just a sort of a lean against it if it wasn't shut properly for the door to swing open. I don't have a peep hole but I've got a very big front window and I can normally see who's at the front door. And if the situation is such that I can't see who's at the front door and I don't really like the sound of it or if I'm not expecting someone, I will go upstairs and look out the window, open the window and see who's there.

ANTICIPATING DANGER AND AVOIDING VIOLENCE

In general, to act sensibly we take measures to minimise risk. Doing so recognises the random and sometimes not-so-random features of everyday violence. Unfortunately, we are not always able to avoid danger despite all our efforts. Eileen states:

> If I went out to a pub or disco, wherever, at night, I drove back and didn't drink. Or I arranged that I could get there and back or knew I was with people I could get home with or get back to their place and stay [there overnight]. I have never been [in the situation] where I have been out and not known I could get home. I took all the general precautions, like not opening the door, always knowing who was on the other side of the door before opening it, especially at night when there's no people around. All those precautions I took. I didn't expect that somebody I had met two or three times would . . . who had been in my home, who had been invited into my home, would do this [rape] to me, after having known him.

After such a life-threatening experience, Eileen reacted like many others who feel their safety is shattered. She withdrew from her friends and family, rarely went out or into the room where the rape occurred and eventually moved from the home where she was once comfortable, but which had become a daily reminder of her vulnerability to danger.

While many take precautions, others are surprised by immediate threats and sudden experiences of violence. Louise, a 62-year-old woman living in London, remarks:

> You see it [stories of violence] in the local [newspaper], but you don't know the people and it's not on this estate [housing complex]. I used to think how awful it was but you think that it is never going to happen to you, don't you?

EVERYDAY VIOLENCE

Keeping violence at bay is an active process. We change our everyday habits, develop elaborate precautionary strategies, and hope for the best.

One of the ways in which people often contend with everyday danger is to find a place where threats seem distant. A rural area, a middle-class community or a wealthy suburb, many believe, provide a refuge from the stranger who is typically associated with potential danger. In the next chapter, people describe their perceptions of how safe they feel their neighbourhood to be. Throughout, these descriptions rely on the steadfast image of the assailant as an intruder who imposes danger from the outside. But danger, commonly confronted in private, lingers in people's memories.

Chapter three
SEARCHING FOR A SAFE PLACE

[I] was aware of crime but it was literally down across the tracks or some place up the country or off, in wherever, up in the hills. It was contained in another place.

I just feel safe here. When we go out we usually leave one of the doors unlocked. Perhaps I shouldn't, but we just do.

Margaret, speaking first, remembers her childhood surroundings as safe, away from danger. Later she recalls being attacked in her barn by a cousin who worked as a farm hand. Margaret's definition of crime differs from her definition of danger. She does not associate this attack, and her memories of being molested by a store keeper, with how she perceives neighbourhood safety. Her reflections on her childhood assaults do not easily match with her images of real criminals – the bank robbers, stealthy burglars or masked strangers. Her feelings about who might harm her continue to be linked with a faceless assailant.

Gail, after moving from a economically and racially mixed area located near a main urban thoroughfare, feels secure in her new home, located in the 'nice' part of a city in central Massachusetts. She would never have left her door unlocked in the other house. Prostitutes seemed a permanent feature of the main street, their customers purchasing pizzas until the early hours of the morning and many street people wandering about. Crime, to both women, is linked to the intended actions of strangers who linger on the 'bad side' of town or who frequent public areas. Both sought the safety of middle-class communities to reduce their anxiety about danger.

Many people are able to choose to live in wealthier communities because of the buffers to street crime and to the intrusion of strangers. Nowadays, those of us who can, do so, juggling the advantages and disadvantages of living in particular neighbourhoods based on our needs for transporation, shopping, children's education and other factors that affect our quality of life. We know about what type of housing we can afford or we stretch ourselves financially to live in a desired spot.

Margaret, a Massachusetts resident of an affluent area for 27 years, recalls:

> I selected the neighbourhood because of its convenience to schools and small shopping areas, and friends and relatives. It felt like a safe neighbourhood and also it seemed like a good neighbourhood to raise my children when they were young. It used to be a very close neighbourhood. Many people with similar values had children and in many of the same instances were probably interested in education and success. So it was a very easy neighbourhood because we seemed to have many of the same rules for our children growing up and everyone took an interest in the other families. So that if I allowed my children out to play I knew that the woman next door or the father, whoever, because they were very good that way, would kind of keep an eye [out] and I would keep an eye on their children. And we had the nicest children in the neighbourhood.

Women and men living in middle-class areas associate their communities with the safety of private space. Danger, it is assumed, can be kept at bay because strangers can be identified. Lynn, in describing her feelings about her neighbourhood, points to the importance of knowing her neighbours in order to boost her feelings of security.

> Well, it's mostly single family or two family houses [here]. And there's not really much crime in the area at all. You know, it's not a place where you have to worry about walking out into your back yard at night and, you know, having somebody jump over the fence or something like that. It's just, I just feel very safe. And it could be, too, because I have a family living in the house [that I feel safe]. An attorney that I went to law school with is now moving into the third floor which should be really fun too as it is a guy that I know. I don't know if it's a false sense of security, but I feel like it's a very safe neighbourhood.

One middle-class expectation is that neighbours contribute to the overall well-being of each other. The 'good' neighbour keeps watch for potential trouble. Sylvia states:

> I feel like I'm part of the neighbourhood, but at a very low level . . . Nobody hangs around with each other. Everybody is sort of 'Hi, how are you doing?' or some people are. Not all the neighbours speak. I mean, some are unfriendly and that's fine because you don't need to be friendly with everyone. Yeah, I'd say I feel like I'm part of the neighbourhood. It has been a safe neighbourhood. I keep saying to myself, law of averages shows that at some point they'll [dangerous people] strike here, which, you know, sometimes makes me nervous. Because I feel like we should be going to get it at some point. And because I have two glass sliding doors in this house, sometimes [I feel vulnerable]. I certainly don't lay awake at nights worrying about it, but I'm conscious about it. I think one reason it has been safe is because it is a neighbourhood of primarily much

> older couples or young couples with little kids. They're pretty much trapped in their homes, whichever group you want to look at. So older people stay in a lot. Now, my neighbours across the street travel a fair amount, but when they're not travelling they're in that house. They don't go out partying at night. They don't care to go out to dinner. They appear to have people in for dinner. And they will disappear for two or three weeks at a time travelling, but when they're here, they're here, and when they're not there are people watching the house. And when we're not here, they watch my house. And you know, people do watch each other's houses in this neighbourhood.

By being conscious that her home is vulnerable, Sylvia recognises the uncertainty of her safety. Unlike Gail, who feels safe in her home with sliding glass doors and amongst residents who watch out for each other, Sylvia knows how danger may 'strike'. Despite her own fear of a former partner, Sylvia locates the danger outside. Even some people in the 'best of neighbourhoods' anticipate violence and guard against it. Judy also relies on those around her, in times of trouble.

> I feel a part of my immediate neighbourhood. The houses are real close to me. I feel OK living here. They [the neighbours] know a little about each other, a little too much for my comfort. But I like my neighbours and it's just safe here. If I felt threatened, part of my plan is I would involve my neighbours. So in that sense I would not live where there was no one in reach if I was alone.

Having neighbours to turn to provides added assurance for many middle-class home-dwellers. Yet, I cannot help but notice the spreading displays of burglar alarms in the affluent areas of town or in the serene suburbs.

These communities are certainly not untouched by 'outside' intrusion. Pristine homes, nestled in areas that are silent, except for the buzz of landscape gardeners cutting grass and pruning shrubs, are wired for security – they are big business for the security industry. The benefits of good schools and manicured lawns do not always include safety. Margaret's neighbourhood, still considered a desirable location for schools and quality of life, has changed for her in recent years. While she no longer has the close relationships with her neighbours, many of whom have moved since their children have grown, she has also been burgled.

> I thought I was very safe until about four years ago. That's the first time I was broken into, and I've been broken into four times. I guess I don't feel that it is as safe. I think it was the kind of place that if I forgot to lock my door I didn't get frantic about it, but now I go around and check the locks. Practically every house has been broken into, to the point that we had as many as five unmarked police cruisers up and around at one point [trying to deter burglars].

A staunchly middle-class neighbourhood, there is no visible street life here. The front lawns are well-kept. For Margaret, the physical surroundings are virtually unchanged over 27 years. What has changed is how she feels about her own safety. The burglaries prompted her not only to alter the physical security of the house, but to reconsider her behaviour inside the house as well. She explains:

> Very recently I opened the door without thinking in the middle of the day and after I had opened it, there was a strange man standing there and it really frightened me a bit. He was supposed to be a salesman. He was trying to sell soap or something, but I got [very uneasy]. All of a sudden I [said to myself] 'What did you do that for?' And I really got angry at myself,

and when I got angry at myself I started yelling at him. And he was nice and polite. He left and there was no problem. I just said I didn't want any [soap] and he started giving me a line and I said, 'Look, I'm not interested.' But it really startled me to find this person standing there and, as I say, knowing that I opened the door so readily. [I had] gotten away from that [habit]. I'll have to look [next time before I open the door].

Margaret no longer takes evening strolls around her neighbourhood. Soon, she sighed, she will sell her house, probably to others like herself – people who want to live in a safe neighbourhood.

Judy, who spoke earlier about feeling more secure with neighbours close at hand, is aware that danger is not that far away from her secluded, lakeside residence:

There's an occasional break in [here]. Very, very rare. It's more apt to be kids coming down by the lake, not even kids, but older teenagers, young adults. Some of them are drinking beer, partying late at night, that kind of thing, not even [committing] crime. But enough so that I see the remnants of them being here. I'm very reluctant to walk too far around the lake. I'm real cautious about doing that alone. They [the kids] camp out, sometimes at night, and I'm real careful about walking around alone. I would never go to bed without locking my door.

Threat lingers with faceless beach dwellers or burglars. It is not unusual, however, that the burglar or the beach dweller is a neighbour's child, or a friend or acquaintance. By avoiding public areas, people feel they can regulate danger by limiting contact with strangers.

Sylvia, who describes the neighbourhood she grew up in as safe, remembers:

SEARCHING FOR A SAFE PLACE

> In the country, ironically, I probably felt safe but again, I remember a guy next door who used to expose himself and he tried getting in the house a couple of times when I was alone. So actually, it wasn't safe, although it seemed safe . . . As a teenager, I grew a little afraid of the guy next door and I used to make sure the door was locked all the time. And I ended up having to call the police one night. My uncle wouldn't allow it. This was someone he had grown up with and I guess in his view it was something you just tolerate . . . We don't turn in neighbours.

Indecent exposure is a criminal offence, but in this instance the neighbour's actions will not be considered a crime. We do not know how often threatening behaviour of acquaintances, friends, relatives and here, long-standing neighbours, come to the attention of the police or justice system. Sylvia's uncle insisted she not label her neighbour's behaviour as criminal offence – that would have been unneighbourly.

Yet the façade of security remains in middle-class, suburban or rural locales. People intentionally move there to feel safer. Gail Counsell, real estate editor of the *Independent* newspaper, states in a recent interview in the *Sunday Times* that security, rather than investment value, was the primary consideration in the purchase of her flat in Hampstead, London. She describes the location in terms of its providing limited access to intruders and the 'short, reassuringly well-lit walk from the tube station.' She was the only woman of the five editors interviewed for an article about how real estate editors choose where to live. She is the only one to mention her security as closely linked to her choice of housing.

Images of danger become subtly woven into our perceptions about a place or community block. For those who live in 'dangerous' places, middle-class areas become meccas of reassurance. Maria, a ten-year resident of an urban housing project, describes her quest for safer housing in a middle-class community when her children were threatened:

> Everything has changed, you know, to be honest with you, that [housing project] is not a place to bring up a child because everything has changed. Instead of getting better it got worse . . . New faces made you feel unsafe. The kids [used to] play outside without being harassed. We could walk outside the neighbourhood at night without being afraid. After about five years, you couldn't leave your door open anymore even if you were sitting in front of the house. You are afraid and that's why the projects is [sic] not the greatest place to raise your child. Why, because it starts nice and dandy when you first move in then it's like you don't trust anyone; you are always looking out the window to see if the kids are fine. You are afraid of teenagers coming around and hitting the kids or taking things away from the kids. You are afraid all the time. Sometimes you don't let your kids play outside because of that fear. In any project here in [central Massachusetts] is not safe for your kids. I was very scared for my daughter because one teenager took out a knife and threatened her with it. That's when I said I have to move out of here. I was afraid for the safety of my daughter. The kids were always harassed by teenagers when they were walking from school and I move out of there fast. I needed to give my kids a new environment where they felt safe.

Crime surveys, in measuring how many people become victims of crime, find that those living in inner city areas, multiracial areas or areas populated by the economically disadvantaged report higher levels of 'fear of crime' and victimisation.[1] These surveys commonsensically define crime as the actions of strangers. Typically victimised more often by burglaries, racial assaults and harassment, drug sales, assaults, vandalism, thefts and street robberies, residents are often attacked by their neighbours and their friends. Street crime, clearly more of a threat in an area which is demoralised by poverty and which is a centre for an illegal, underground economy, brings more potential danger and the residents are aware of this ever-present threat.

Popularised in song and story, the 'bad side' of town evokes images of everyday violence. Unsafety lurks on the street as part of an active illicit drug market, or part of the trade in prostitution, or as part of an overspill of disputes between friends and family. The residents know that not all their neighbours are dangerous, but some certainly are. Cynthia, living in a public housing estate in central Massachusetts, has a good idea of the dangers posed by forms of crime in her neighbourhood.

> Some of the people who live here now . . . are junkies, dope pushers . . . and you never know what they are going to do when you walk down the street. There could be a desperado junky that could jump on you, stab you, do whatever they'll have to do to get some money for a fix. You know it's a lot of crazy people out there and a lot of them are right in here. See, they like to bring other kind of people [here], like people that like to break into apartments and their minds are working bad 24 hours a day.

Ricardo, another resident of a housing project in central Massachusetts, sees much of the illicit activity which takes place in his neighbourhood:

> In the area I live there is drugs, prostitution, a lot of drinking and marijuana, loud parties where they give drugs and alcohol to minors and a lot of robberies.

Street life linked with the wheeling and dealing of illegal and quasi-legal markets means that violence is more visible. Ed, who admits to routinely carrying a hand weapon, feels that his neighbourhood is unsafe because of street activity, in which he himself participates:

'Cause there's a lot of crazy people running around. Incredibly crazy people. People who are psychologically deranged, who have very little money, who are desperate and destitute and very depressed and dangerous. They do crazy things. They, well, they shot one guy. Just shot a guy down the street. They say it wasn't drug related, but it doesn't matter what the cause was, it just happened here. A friend of mine watched a friend of his get shot in the head over a crazy argument. I think you get a lot of this in the inner city and I shouldn't expect there to be anything different. But living in a city like this [in central Massachusetts] you see everything a little bit closer.

Within these areas of active street life, violence might arise when deals are broken or someone cheats. Violence is also used to ensure compliance to deals or to discipline a careless worker in the underground ecomony. Violence is the end of an argument or a part of the negotiation. And its effects boil over into the wider community, to those who do not participate.

Bea, who lives in an area in central Massachusetts that has a reputation for its high crime rate, describes her constant reminders of danger:

We've lived in this house for six years. We lived up the street from this house for the first two or three years, I guess since we were married. And I used to walk by this house. It was vacant. And I just kind of fell in love with it. We knew the street wasn't marvellous, but in all the time we lived there we didn't really have any problems except trying to park in the winter. So we bought this house, like ten houses down from where we were. When I said because we lived up there, there were no problems and so we felt safe in buying the house. There were a lot of problems. [They were burgled four times.] Last year was the first quiet summer. We still have drug dealing. We still have prostitutes. But they do all that quietly. We also have half-way houses, those are fine. [Do you feel comfortable in the neighbourhood?] I walk back and forth right now because we only have one vehicle at this present time, and I'm doing that walking in the daylight. Am I comfortable? No, because I have to walk at a fast pace. If I walk at a slow pace, people, you know, stop. You are not allowed to walk, just walk – you must be moving. If you look like you are busy, they don't think you're out there [working the streets]. And mind you, I've got my coat on, and obviously I'm on my way somewhere. I've got my hands in my pockets. But no, I can't walk there. I can't walk back and forth leisurely because it's amazing. Just last week I had to wait for a bus and this one car was on its third trip when it dawned on me to get the [licence] plate number. By then, of course, he [the kerb crawler] didn't come back.

Despite the greater number of police deployed in high crime areas, activities such as drug sales and street prostitution often take place in full view of the residents in the neighbourhood. Local women are targets for men soliciting prostitutes. Whilst there may be periodic police 'sweeps' of visible crime in the area, street life is an integral part of a local economy as well as an integral part of the local residents' knowledge about how to spot danger. Some of the participants in the illegal economy may even be viewed by local residents as protectors or may succeed in intimidating residents so that they do not call the police when violence occurs or when the drug market is operating on the street.

Discrimination by class and by race serves to maintain the pockets of geographical danger. Commonly, the poor and minorities, and the areas they inhabit, become synonymous with danger and violence. When we label a 'place' as dangerous, we include images of assailants and their racial stereotypes as the strangers who are dangerous. Those living in 'no go' areas do so because they find that these are the few places they can afford to live or where landowners will rent them accommodation. Publicly subsidised housing is most likely to be isolated in less affluent areas. Living in an area with highly visible criminal street activity takes its toll on residents who are ever alert for danger. The spectrum of drug-related activity, a thriving business these days, triggers violence connected with the use and sale of drugs, along with the possible robbery and theft committed by addicts needing money for an immediate fix. Patti, a 28-year-old resident of a city on the US Eastern seaboard, states:

> All the streets down the hill is all druggies and stuff, so that's unsafe. But I don't know it [I consider] that part of the neighbourhood . . .

Safety is illusive within an area with an active street economy, even for the urban middle class. Jill, a member of neighbourhood watch in inner London, notes:

> We found a house and a place of work conveniently situated and we could afford it. So I suppose having been here for a while you get used to it and therefore you like it because it's familiar. I like the park across the road. Neighbours in the square which actually forms the resident's association are very friendly, supportive, and glad that we've moved into this house because this house was empty for a long, long time and posed a bit of a threat. You wave at people, they stop and chat. That's nice. [Do you feel this is a safe neighbourhood?] Not especially. There is a striking imbalance around here of homeowners who are professionals and obviously they bought [homes] here because this is what they could afford. They might not have two cents to rub together, but at least they have a kind of life style that is different. We have here a tiny middle-class pocket sandwiched between two huge estates with a lot of, dare we call

them, 'problem families' in them. So I'm very conscious of that.

Being conscious of one's surroundings, alert for trouble, may not automatically mean one feels safe or unsafe. Safety and feelings of safety as well as danger arise in different contexts, at varying times. Areas that seem safe to outsiders may be perceived by residents as troublesome, or those that seem dangerous to outsiders may feel comfortable, or at least manageable to others. Mike states:

> [Do you feel it's a safe neighbourhood?] It's a hard one [to answer]. It's safer than some but yet it's not one in which women walk alone at night. It's safe in terms of days. And nights, it's like it gets confusing. I think generally I feel fairly safe there. What's confusing is that feeling safe has a lot to do with previous experience and it doesn't. I think the feeling of [possibly] getting mugged [in the neighbourhood] is there.

Mike demonstrates how feelings of safety ebb and flow. With darkness comes uncertainty about one's ability to spot danger. Public places that seem safe during the day perhaps become threatening at night.

Day or night, some people avoid some public places because they feel that those places are always potentially dangerous. Fred, for example, never uses public toilets.

> I've been terrified of men's rooms. Especially in places where men are apt to congregate, just because that was the place where I used to get beat up the most.

Fred's wariness of public toilets, though, is linked to his experiences of being beaten in the toilet by school mates. While he treats a public space as potentially dangerous, his experience of danger comes from his relationships with former classmates. Laura, raped by a date, is uneasy about buying cigarettes in all-night convenience stores:

Last week I was driving [alone] and I have this feeling about driving at night. I think this might have to do with the fact that I just recently got my licence, but I was going to this convenience store, and I was thinking about the fact that I was alone, and that it was dark, and going to a convenience store – you hear about things that happen late at night at convenience stores, so yeah, I was very conscious [about my safety].

Police and security experts are aware of people's concern about random violence. They spend a great deal of time advising us about safety and how to avoid becoming a victim of crime. Their approach to safety encourages individual action to minimise personal risk. Typically, they suggest that homes be fortified by trustworthy locks and bolts, and that adequate precaution be exercised when out in public places.

Whilst the police are right to recognise people's quest for individual safety, they promote community cooperation in the fight against crime in order to reduce people's anxiety without any regard to potential danger *within* communities. These efforts, and the accompanying advice about sensible precaution in the public sector, focus police crime prevention programmes on the dangers posed by the stranger. Unfortunately, the advice does not take into account the everyday nature of safety and danger, it does not tap into the many strategies people already use to negotiate danger, and it ignores the fact that people typically know the person who frightens and threatens them.

Safety advice now appears everywhere. When I visit the public library, police posters remind me to keep an eye on my belongings. Women's magazines and local newspapers provide tips about how to avoid becoming a victim of a purse snatching or mugging. Insurance companies send householders suggestions for adequate security devices to prevent burglaries. Television programmes, such as *Crimewatch* in the UK or *Unsolved Mysteries* and *911* in the US, show reconstructions of criminal events and give viewers information about how crime occurs. Even the newsletter from my health insurer includes a page about safety, suggesting that 'Safety at night means being aware of the possibility of crime.'

Minimising risk of criminal victimisation, we are told by police and crime prevention specialists, is the responsibility of each individual. Crime prevention literature, targeted primarily at women, children and the elderly, acknowledges our anxiety about criminal violence and attempts to reassure us that the actual incidence of violent crime is low. None the less, in order to promote a feeling of greater security, the following suggestions are typically forwarded by police:

- When at home: keep doors locked at all times; have mortice or dead-bolt locks installed; windows should have proper catches and locks; ask callers for identification, especially utility workers; install and use a peep hole and chain on the door; keep a radio on when out of the house; do not let mail and newspapers accumulate if away, have a neighbour collect them.
- When out in public: keep valuables close to your body; avoid dimly lit streets and alleyways; sit next to conductors or guards on public transportation; check your car before you enter it.

People are told, in great detail, how crime occurs and how they, as individuals, can personally reduce the opportunity for crime. If people frequent places that are known to be dangerous or they do not follow exactly the rules for precaution, then we implicitly hold them responsible for whatever happens to them. Take, for instance, the public reaction to a recent, highly publicised violent crime. A 28-year-old woman went jogging one evening in Central Park in April 1989 and was attacked, beaten and raped by a gang of young lads 'out for a good time'. While many expressed outrage about the vicious assault, there was a recurring question, articulated by a passer-by interviewed for the radio. He stated that he was both sad and angry about the attack. Sad for the woman and her family; angry because the woman 'put herself in the position to be attacked'. After all, doesn't everyone know and accept the fact that Central Park is dangerous, especially at night?

And we expect sensible people, particularly women, to follow prudent rules of self-restriction as evidence of their caution. Police advise women to take special care in public places and adopt an alert, confident manner when alone on the street. No doubt, until this event, this woman and the thousands of other women and men who exercise in Central Park had heard about the 'dangers' of the park. Obviously, she and those others felt safe enough to jog and probably developed techniques to spot danger. However beneficial in the past, her safety strategies are not helpful against a large gang of young men determined to cause injury and havoc. Few strategies are likely to be successful against such odds.

As the danger of public settings continues to attract the attention of the media, our concern remains focused on guarding personal safety in public places or on fortifying the locks and bolts of our own homes. 'Danger' thus becomes identified with a place and avoiding a potentially dangerous place is considered good common sense. Many people can already name specific places they would never go to or areas where they would never park their cars, live, accept employment, or spend leisure time. Places such as elevators, multi-storey car parks, bus stops or open fields have reputations for harbouring undesirables, stereotypically men, who may harm.

The image of the danger of the public and the silence around the danger of the private is a solid fixture in our knowledge about crime. It is woven into our lessons about danger and safety that we acquire throughout our lifetimes. Crime, and what we define as crime, differs from danger. We turn now to an examination of our lessons about danger.

Chapter four
ON LEARNING SAFETY AND DANGER

How do we learn about protecting ourselves from violence? How do we go about gathering our many rules of thumb for safety? While some people are merely collectors of information, others find out about danger from painful and lasting memories of threat and violation. What happens if we have to alter the safe to unsafe, when danger suddenly erupts from an apparently trustworthy place or person?

Throughout our lives, we learn about safety from a variety of sources: direct involvement, observation, and the shared knowledge of family, friends, teachers, peers and co-workers. There are those who describe childhoods devoid of any consideration for danger. They grow up in supportive, secure households with little or no tension or animosity. They also report never being frightened of adults or peers, at least not that they can remember. Indeed, some people are surprised that they are unable to recall even the emotions of worry or fear during their childhood years. Others, who recollect feeling basically safe, tell of incidents of occasional danger. These experiences often have significant effects on later choices about cautionary behaviour. Even though they are passed off as minor events, none the less they remain scary. Still others report living in households which pose continuous threats to them. These people are subjected to physical and/or sexual abuse largely from their fathers or other close male relatives or family members. And finally, there are those who lived in dangerous neighbourhoods, attending schools where bullies rule the playgrounds and crime taints the overall quality of life.

Lessons in childhood raise an awareness about safety in those children. Researchers now acknowledge the often lifelong memories and pain caused by childhood physical and sexual abuse. These experiences offer a child lasting information about violence and danger. There is no certainty, though, that particular events have any specific effect on adults' attitudes towards their own security. People do come to terms with their pasts and subsequently understand the world in different ways. However, it is likely that these experiences do contribute to an overall understanding of one's relationship to personal safety. Even though the weight given to an individual instance may be small, it is important to recognise the complexities of learning about protection, the cumulative effect of many events and how people themselves make sense of them.

Direct experiences of violence or danger as teenagers and adults either confirm or call into question childhood lessons. For example, a woman, who when small never considered the possibility of being sexually unsafe, must immediately think about it after being threatened on a date or by a boyfriend. Men who characteristically report feeling secure suddenly consider themselves vulnerable after experiencing a serious physical assault. And some adults, particularly women, do not actually ever expect to feel totally safe. While our own pasts do not comprise all our information about personal safety, some experiences, especially those which are directly life-threatening, will have a long term, if not permanent, effect. Adjusting to a different orientation of self-protection is typically reported by both women and men who have confronted these forms of violence.

Safe-keeping information is gained through observation of or exposure to violence experienced by others. People like the police, social workers, battered women or rape support workers, doctors, school counsellors and probation officers may work with clients who experience much brutality in their everyday lives. Those who have only an indirect involvement with danger look at first-hand reports to make assessments both of their own safety and that of others. Some also use this information to draw up additional precautionary rules to avoid violence ever happening to them.

Safe-keeping, a continuous process of risk assessment, involves understanding that you are potentially susceptible to violence both as an individual and as member of a particular group. The gay man who knows that most of his friends have been either verbally or physically assaulted because they are homosexual will take additional safety precautions. A woman, constantly bombarded by news accounts of rapes, abductions and abuses, locates herself amongst those vulnerable simply because she is a woman. Hearing about racial attacks provokes caution in someone likely to feel in similar peril. Our cumulative information about danger shapes our strategies for preserving our own safety. We begin in childhood.

CHILDHOOD LESSONS

Children learn about personal safety through all aspects of their lives. Some people do not have any childhood memories of specific measures being taken for personal safety. They describe living in homes where no one encountered threats or experiences of violence, attending schools without bullying, and living in neighbourhoods where children seldom confronted one another. Many of these, however, did recall being taught how to lock their front doors, but not being told why they must do so. Others were given the standard warnings about avoiding strangers. What is surprising, particularly for someone who remembers no frightening experiences as a child, is the large number of people who could recollect either actual or threatened violence – events which happened in their own homes or neighbourhoods, at school, as well as outside their immediate areas.

EVERYDAY VIOLENCE

Unsafety at Home

Inside our homes we are taught what precautions to take against the possibility of intrusion by outsiders. Some, however, must also learn how to protect themselves from those inside. Bea, who grew up in a small town in Central Massachusetts, spoke with great pain about her childhood. The terror resided in her house. Her father, physically violent and sexually threatening, looms large as her first teacher about unsafety.

> I have no idea what age I was. I can only guess that probably some of it. . . I've put it away. I do know the sister that's next to me, I can remember her as being very tiny. Whether I saw her as very tiny because we were all involved . . . I was 15 when I called the police. How anybody would set him off, that was something you'd never know. I mean, the initial thing you never knew. Later you knew, sure, if you were just going to let him beat up on you and so and so, that you would be OK. It's hard to explain. I knew that, that [reference to sexual threats] wasn't normal for him to be running around like that. So a part of me knew there was something wrong, but I didn't know sexually. I didn't know. I guess I knew I had to tell my mother. But why I knew I had to tell her that he was running around naked, I didn't know what the reason was. I knew there was fright there, but I do not know how to describe it as sexual fright because I didn't know. I had to go through a lot of years of counselling to deal with it. It wasn't until years later . . . I had no idea just where my thinking had gone. I do know through all my early adult years, all through my 20s, I wished this man dead with such a passion. If you told me his funeral was tomorrow, you weren't breaking my heart. [In addition to] dealing with that I had to deal with the guilt because he was my father. My mother always felt it was nobody's business what went on in the home. And I'll never know if she

had finally changed her mind. That day [I called the police] I was threatening to call regardless of what she said, but at the last minute she did yell, 'OK.' I'll never know if I would have done it on my own. It was a small town. My mother went to school with some of the police officers. She wanted no one, no one, no family to know. No one should know what went on in your home.

One complex dimension of danger in people's private lives is the fusing of fear with shame. The resulting silence about the dangers of private space contributes to the continual emphasis on the dangers of public space. Sylvia recalls feeling sexually threatened as a teenager by an uncle with whom she was living.

He [my uncle] made me feel sexually threatened. Again, I wasn't clear on what that was about, but by the time I was that age, I knew it was not OK; I mean, unlike with the man in the basement [who molested me when I was real little], I had no idea what that was. But with my uncle I knew it wasn't OK and I knew that when he would say certain things to me and try to touch me, that I spent most of my two years between 16 and 17 planning so that I would never be home alone with him if I could help it. Which was hard because my aunt ran a dancing school and she was often not there. And you know it made it hard. But I got really clever at bringing girlfriends home. I shared it with one of my close girlfriends. So she went home with me a lot to make sure that I was OK. And in the sense it was sort of an adventure when she was with me. But for me it was dread. It was real dread. You know, and I was just dreading being caught alone with him [my uncle]. But once I had my first boyfriend, it ceased. Just a change in his behaviour. And I stopped feeling unsafe as I had. I was always cautious. And I never felt totally OK. But I didn't feel as if I walked in the house and he was there by himself I didn't feel as 'oh, no'.

Research studies indicate that girls, more so than boys, are likely to experience some kind of intrusive sexual experience before they turn 18. Liz Kelly, a leading British expert on childhood sexual abuse, suggests that the figures vary widely, depending on how researchers classify and count unwanted sexual experiences. Estimates of the levels of abuse experienced by girls and by boys range from 1 in every 2 girls and 1 in every 5–6 boys to 1 in 6–8 girls and 1 in 10–20 boys. What is equally as interesting is that it is virtually impossible to find comparable figures of physical abuse, often the accompanying evil, that separate out estimates by sex.[1] Mike, whose father died when he was barely 4, leaving a widow with four children, speaks of the physical abuse he experienced.

> I had a difficult time. There was a real cycle of violence. I was the oldest boy and my mother would hit me and I would hit them and she would hit me. She used to have a 2 x 4 [large stick] on top of the refrigerator which she would use or threaten to use when I wouldn't listen. Seeing my brothers crying and in the corner or getting hit was probably the most upsetting thing in the long run. And that went on until I was 13 or so, when I left for the seminary.

Leo, who is currently serving a life sentence for murder and is also a convicted rapist, recalls his violent childhood.

> They [my parents] were continually on at each other. She was always cursing him and threatening to leave him and these kinds of things. And there was a lot of rage, there was a lot of physical stuff. Not to the point where she ever had to be hospitalised or anything. It was a constant going at each other physically. I had to climb on an end table when I was very small and I took a candlestick. And my father was there. He had just gotten through hitting my mother and he was now

screaming at her. I hit him and cracked his head with that. And then I had to leave immediately. I used to have to do a lot of that stuff like that, hit him with something and leave. And then I'd run into the woods and they'd get the police. By that time things had quieted down so I wasn't to get a direct assault on me. I'd get it later. That's a frightening kind of thing because I was only a little kid and he was a grown man. So I learned to assault somebody very early. I found out with my father that as long as I struck back and acted out real violently quickly and then could get away from him, things would be a lot easier for me. I got to be about 13 when I became what they considered incorrigible.

Judy also reports being afraid in her own home:

I have felt threatened by the man that brought me up. He's no longer alive. I wonder how he would feel about knowing how very frightened I felt with him sometimes. He beat the shit out of me. I was just afraid of his physical power. It doesn't feel like a beating. It feels like he held a physical threat over me that I was just afraid to go beyond a certain point which was not a very big line to cross. When I was 16 he broke a chair over my back. He also threw me across the room. It hurt. I ran out of the house.

Unlike Leo, Judy could not fight back. She continues:

I would have never fought back. It never occurred to me. Never. But it always occurred to me to protect myself until I was afraid he would hurt himself and then protecting myself had absolutely no meaning if it meant that he would be hurt.

No doubt physical battles are not unusual events in some households where the tension is high and the confrontations escalate as the children grow older. Safety strategies such as avoidance, verbal negotiation of tensions, monitoring the temper and behaviour of those nearby, using companions for protection, or coming to know certain physical settings as unsafe, are but a few of the skills learnt during childhood.

Unsafety near Home

Children may learn of danger outside their homes in their immediate surroundings. Some remember their childhood neighbourhoods as quiet and peaceful; others grew up in what they considered dangerous, inner-city areas. Whether in the city, a small town or the country, the hazard of potential violence appears in many different forms.

Margaret, from a small town in rural Vermont, recalls feeling threatened as a child, then immediately remembers feeling threatened at work in what should be seemingly safe surroundings.

> I was living on the farm and it happened to be a relative. We were in the horse barn and he opened his trousers and tried to pull me down in the hay. I do not have a great sense of being threatened but I was upset about it and ran to tell my mother. She went out. I was probably 7 years old. She had a bat with her. I think he left. I think she sent him back home. I think for a while I was kind of apprehensive in the barn. Whoever was there, the hired man, I think, I probably kept my distance. I think maybe in that respect, and maybe in some ways, I think I always went with a sense of being ready, just in case. Avoid dark alleys, walk in the middle of the road, safe where it's lighted, be careful where you park your car. I think there was always that kind of watching. I also worked in a hospital and I used to have to work nights. I was on call. And worked at what is University Hospital now. I always was very cautious about walking down the middle of the corridor when I was working nights,

ON LEARNING SAFETY AND DANGER

> about 1.00 in the morning. Because there were always stories about people being hauled into linen closets. And I know it did happen. I always stayed away from the residents and interns who had that reputation. I think it had some influence on it [my caution]. Because, I mean, it was a sudden kind of thing and these are the [feelings you remember]. I kind of remember now about getting hauled in [at the hospital]. It was someone I knew. I was walking at night and the next thing I knew, it was dark and there was a bed and I just pushed him away. This was at the hospital. I remember going in as a child with another young friend. We must have been very young, 7 or 8. It was a candy store. We were visiting my aunt. It was up in town, the town I lived in and it was a soda shop. I remember one of the owners trying to put his arm around me and hold me, you know, put his hand on my breast. That upset me and I never told anyone about it until later years. I guess I was upset that this older man did that. Whereas I guess I wasn't as upset with this relative who was the hired hand who was younger and I knew that he had been in trouble. But I think an older man who had respect really bothered me a great deal.

Children are taught to stay away from strangers. When a respectable adult is threatening and untrustworthy, a child may have a difficult time assessing who is safe and who is unsafe. Sylvia illustrates this when she describes the neighbourhood in which she grew up.

> I really do not know. It's hard for me to remember. I mean I shouldn't have felt safe in the city homes, if I did it was because I didn't know any better. But I do not think they were safe places to live at all.

Sylvia had to contend with her uncle with whom she lived and later with a neighbour who exposed himself to her. She felt apprehensive each time she was alone in her house with her uncle. And, she adds, in general she felt secure in her neighbourhood.

Moving house for some also brings drastic changes in how a child manages threats. Peter, a 28-year-old Central Massachusetts resident, comments about the stark difference between two of his homes as a boy.

> Think of going to a nice little school where you played little league and stuff like that. Being uprooted from that. Your parents being divorced and you being put into a neighbourhood where you had to walk your sister to the local pizza parlour because of the prostitutes working on the street. Wouldn't you think that that was a drastic change? They [the prostitutes] used to hang on the wall at the end of the street. They did that ten years ago, and they did that fifty years ago, and they're doing it now. There was a lot of drugs. There were small gang fights here and there, but they usually didn't amount to anything. They were racial fights, between blacks and Puerto Ricans. The cops would pull up and see us all with baseball bats and beers, and they'd say, 'Keep it clean' and drive away. When they said 'Keep it clean', they meant no knives, that's all. Either you took part in the fights or you just went home. Some kids never went out. They just went home after school. They just stayed home. They got picked on all the way home, sometimes all the way to school. It even happens in the small towns, at a different calibre.

Neighbourhood kids can also constitute a threat. Fred recalls his anguish about being on the receiving end of such abuse.

> I was constantly getting beaten up by the other kids. It was a constant terror. I was afraid to go to the bus stop. I was afraid to walk to school. I was afraid to go to the store. You know, 'cause it was always bigger

boys. Actually, no, there was Joanne. She used to hit me in her garage and beat the shit out of me. She was big. They used to call me 'fairy' and 'fag'. That's when I didn't know what the words meant. That's when I was, like, 5 and 6 years old.

Most of the men and some of the women reported that it was in confrontations with other children that they learnt to match violence, like with like. Rivalries with other schools, neighbourhoods or gangs as well as skirmishes in the playground and on the way to and from home primed many, particularly the men, with knowledge about how, who and when to fight. Sticking up for yourself, or learning to be a bully, are lessons in keeping safe as an adult. Gordon states:

Well, our house had been broken into a couple of times when I was growing up. I knew of other houses [that had been burgled]. I knew of people that were beaten up. But the beating part was mostly the stuff that most kids go through. There were a lot of children. There was a grammar school [in the US, the first eight grades of school, teaching ages 6 to 13] around the corner from my house and it was for my [housing] development, so there were a lot of kids in the neighbourhood. And when you have that many kids, there's always going to be a lot of competition – who's better than who, who's bigger than who, who's stronger than who and the way people usually figure that out is by proving it. I'm not bemoaning some of the shit that I went through as a kid 'cause it toughened me in ways now that might not have if I hadn't gone through that. And I wouldn't go through that again for all the tea in China, no way.

Studies of aggression at school indicate that boys are more likely to be involved than girls. Boys tend towards physical force, while girls use verbal and social manipulation. Deborah speaks of her attempts to avoid harassment at school.

> I rarely went out in the playground. I only had one or two friends. I basically avoided people in my first secondary school. Everybody hated me there. They ripped my clothes off at PE lessons. [They] did it to humiliate me. They were always hiding my clothes. I would try to get to a lesson before everybody else and then leave before everyone else. I just tried to ignore people. I was pretty much upset most of the time the last year in primary school and the first two years of secondary school. It was only the girls who picked on me. Boys never said anything nasty to me.

A 38-year-old London woman recalling her experiences of bullying at school remarked in a recent newspaper interview, 'I'm definitely a bit paranoid, and I hate people being left out of things. Did I tell my mum? No, never. Not a thing.'

These events in children's lives, 'just the usual kids' spats', contribute to our childhood lessons in safety. Ricardo who lives in Central Massachusetts, now 25, bitterly recalls the racial violence he experienced as a child.

> When I was 11 years old we moved to [this city] and I was beat up because I didn't know the language and that put fear in me. It made me take action. I stayed by myself most of the time. I took boxing. I wanted to do more so I learnt martial arts to protect myself against anybody, mostly white people. I had a lot of trouble with whites because I was Puerto Rican. I had just come from Puerto Rico to start a new life, thinking that everything was going to be all right and it turned out to be a disaster. In Puerto Rico, I fought a few times but I knew when it was coming. It was not as damaging as the experiences that I faced here. Over here I worried about getting beaten up, worried about the language. It affected me emotionally and physically. At times, I used to be jumpy when I used to walk around and it made me not trust anybody. I will react violently. I even hit

girls when they talked bad to me and sometimes I felt so angry that I used to hit people for just looking at me with a dead look or making faces at me. I hated all of them [white people] and got even every time any white person did anything to me. It took me a long time to realise that there were some people that were not prejudiced and that [they] didn't have nothing to do with what happened to me when I was 11. But again it took a long time for me to fight that anger out of me.

Two of the men interviewed spent some time in reform schools (borstals) as young adults. There, the harsh realities of institutional life show the glaring contradictions involved in being in a place for 'reform' in which the only lesson was that the most aggressive survive. Leo recalls his experiences in one such notorious prison on the Eastern seaboard of America.

I believe I was just about 14 then. And even though I came off the streets – I came from some pretty rough housing projects and all that craziness – the school for boys was an awakening for me because it was the first time I'd been put in a place where there was a lot of people concentrated in one little small area. I learnt quick. So I learnt real quick in there the weaker ones were assaulted. They were assaulted by staff and other inmates and the ones that were aggressive, you know, and assaulted other people lived half-way decently. At least you could survive without the fear of it. I was still fearful of going into a cottage with maybe 25 or 30 [boys], and in that cottage [there were] different sizes and there were blacks. I had never lived, even though I lived in ghetto areas you might say, blacks and whites were still separated at the time. So not blacks and whites are all mixed up in a small area, in a little cottage, so I had a lot of fears around physical safety. There's no doubt about it. But again, fortunately there was people

> I knew from the same area that I came from that had been there before me so I fit right in with certain people that had been there. Within a few days I had to go into a shower room with somebody and get actually in a fight, a physical thing, and it was broken up. Then I wasn't really bothered after that much any more. I got into fights after that, but they weren't like the type of things that were predatory. They might break out over a pool game or something like that, but other than that, nobody ever took anything from me, you know. . . I was able to survive without becoming the victim. But then I learnt to victimise people. I didn't really care about those people I was victimising either.

Experiencing brutality does not necessarily mean that an individual will respond in the same way in return. 'Attack before you are attacked' is but one way of assuring one's own safety.

Young people who live in what might be considered dangerous neighbourhoods develop the finely-tuned street sense characteristic of adults. Children learn to read the streets for danger signs. Linda, now a resident of Central Massachusetts, recalls the physical environment of her childhood:

> We lived in a terrible housing project in Brooklyn [New York]. [Were you aware of crime at any time in your neighbourhood when you were growing up?] Constantly. [What kinds of crime?] Drugs, murder, assault. Assault happened all the time. Child abuse, robbery. There was a guy in the neighbourhood murdered and they interviewed some people. The housing authority used to harass me for hanging out in the hall. I was cold so I was in the hall. We used to get beaten up a lot. It was a predominantly black neighbourhood and we were white and I think there were residues of tensions still going on. One time we were playing basketball at the local public school and I do not know exactly what

ensued, but somebody called out, 'You black nigger.' Well, we literally had people chasing us home. I ran up to my house. I looked out the window and there were literally fifty people waiting for me to come down. There were the people you knew and the people you didn't know. The people I knew, many of which were black and Hispanic, I felt very safe with. In fact, I sort of relied on them to intervene if anything happened, which they would. But sort of in the larger neighbourhood, I felt very unsafe.

In contrast, others grow up in places where they never confronted serious danger. John describes his surroundings as a child in a Yorkshire village in England:

I lived in a village, you know. I was with my parents and everything was fine. You feel pretty safe. We always locked the doors. It wasn't like a village where you could just leave everything open because it was quite a big village and an awful lot of burglaries in the village. Oh yeah, you locked it [the house], but that was, I suppose, just inbred in me. You had a key and you locked the door. You just did it automatically. You didn't think about it. It didn't go through me head that I was protecting myself every time I locked the door. I just locked the door and went out. My mother used to go out to work, lock the door and put the key in the garden shed on a little ledge. So we knew when we came in from school where the key was.

Jill also assumed that her home in the West Midlands, England, was safe.

Never locked the back door. The back door was hardly locked, even when there was no one in the house. I would look after the family dog when I lived at home and I walked the dog late at night. I used to, when I was 17, go to dances and discos up at the University and walk around on my own at all times of the night. Four in the morning sometimes. Never batted an eyelid at all. Very safe in town. I do not know if it's that safe anymore. [Crime was] something you read about in the local paper, but it was never truly awful. I can remember once or twice when I was 15 my parents went away on holiday and left my sister and myself in the house and we used to lock the back door, shut the windows. That was our concession [to safety].

Unsafety outside the Neighbourhood

Places, as well as specific people or types of people, become labelled as potentially hazardous. Mike, for instance, remembered being approached by a man in a park when he was 11 or 12 years old. 'I just started staying away from the park and I think that [I started] being scared of gay men, or men who look like they may be gay or look like they may look at my body.' Frank remembers feeling apprehensive about attending secondary school in a part of London known to be home to many members of the National Front - a neo-Nazi organisation. As a young black man, he knew that he was visiting hostile territory. The area is demarcated by its graffiti declaring white power and calling for blacks to be 'sent back'.

In recent years, growing concern has focused largely on the threat posed by strangers. Most of us have been told not to accept rides or candy or sweets from those we do not know, to refuse unwanted touches and kisses and to 'say no' to danger. From the recollections of adults, it is clear that children are already saying no through avoidance, negotiation, clever social skills and, in some situations, by fighting back. Rarely are these encounters reported to anyone. And as adults, many come to understand that they have experienced danger merely because they are a 'type' of person: they are women, Hispanic, black, poor, live in the 'wrong' place. Others come to understand that violence can be random, arbitrary, frightening and pointless. Although some acquire physical skills to protect themselves, most try to establish patterns aimed at keeping safe. These are often successful. Yet, despite their best efforts, a number of people experience some threats or violence as adults.

ADULT LESSONS: DIRECT KNOWLEDGE OF VIOLENCE

Those who experience severe violence alter their awareness and routines of safety. Such processes are very much a part of finding an equilibrium where one can feel reasonably safe. Researchers know a great deal about the reactions of those victimised by serious crime.[2] Initially, researchers focused on the devastating effect of rape on women's lives.[3] The cumulative knowledge of crime victims' support systems in the United States and Britain indicates that those who have had life-threatening experiences typically feel fearful about their safety afterwards. Most suffer from some short term disruption of their everyday lives and exhibit a number of symptoms of distress. For a little while, at least, sleep and eating patterns change, as does sexual responsiveness. Fear, anger, distrust, self-blame and embarrassment are also common. Emotional recovery from incidents of extreme violence is directly affected by the support from within the victim's immediate circle. For some, these short-term responses linger on much too long; for a few others, it seems as if their whole life undergoes complete and permanent change.

Within the past few years, researchers are uncovering the commonness of serious violence within intimate and friendship relationships. Few of these incidents of serious violence come to the attention of the police. Because threats and harm arising from dating or family situations are typically considered not to be the law's business by the police as well as by some victims, there is little knowledge about how many people actually experience danger and violence in their lifetimes. When these are added together with brutality committed by strangers, it is clear that many people have had direct experience of violence. Recent estimates in the United States suggest that five out of six adults will experience an attempted or completed violent crime in their lifetimes.[4] Even though they may remain silent about it, the resulting awareness of danger and unsafety filters into most adults' daily routines.

Rape and Sexual Assault

When Eileen was raped in her own home, all her own knowledge about safety was thrown into a turmoil.

> I was always warned as a child not to go with strangers and all the things that parents warn you of. That was part of my upbringing. It wasn't just because I was going into town or something. It was just part of my upbringing. Before we opened the front door to put the safety lock on, always to lock the house, things like that. Obviously we talked, as children, that towns were big things to us. But, you know, although I did grow up in the country, we did go shopping in the town, and we did go to places like Bristol for shopping and appointments and to go out to in the evenings, to the theatre and things like that. So it wasn't as if the town was a place that was in awe to us, because it wasn't. We did go there quite often.

Eileen moved to London when she was 21, sharing a flat with a room-mate. Late on a Sunday, she received a call from an acquaintance she had known for a while asking her out to dinner.

> I said, 'No, it's too late. I [am] going to work in the morning. But why not come round with a bottle of wine?' My flatmate was in at the time, and he came

round and we drank wine, talked. It got to 1 o'clock in the morning. My flatmate said, 'I'm going to bed. I have to get up in the morning.' I was thinking the same thing. You can't be rude and say, 'Just go.' I probably would be now. We just continued talking and then I said, 'Look, it's getting late. I've got to go to bed now. I do not know where you're staying, but I've got to go to work tomorrow.' And the guy informed me that he hadn't made any arrangements to stay anywhere, and that he was probably over the legal limit to drive. So I said, 'Fine, you can stay on the sofa,' and gave him a sleeping bag, blankets, put the sofa together and went off to bed, got changed, got into bed. About five minutes later there's a knock on the door. I got out of bed, put on a dressing gown and went to the door. And it was him. And he said, 'I haven't seen you for a long time,' [and he wanted me to talk to him] and [he was right] I hadn't seen him for a long time. I'd seen him briefly in August, because that's how he got my telephone number, and this happened in January. He said, 'Come out and have a cigarette, I haven't seen you in ages. ' Anything for a quiet life. So I went out, had a cigarette. Then suddenly, he put his hands on me. I said, 'Right, that's it. I'm going to bed now.' He got up behind me.

He raped her at knife-point in the lounge. Eileen continues:

I thought they might say it served me right for letting him into my flat. It sounds a bit strange. So I didn't tell anybody. I realise now that if I had screamed, I might not be here today. I've always maintained that, should anything like that have ever happened to me, I would scream and fight and kick. I just didn't. I was in a daze for a long time. If anybody said, 'Are you OK?' I would have said, 'Yeah, I'm fine.' I wasn't myself, I just carried on. I spent a lot of time in my bedroom, because that's where it didn't happen. The only time I would stay in the lounge was when my flatmate was in the lounge as well. I'd get up and have a bath at half six and go to work. Leave the flat around half past seven, get to work around half past eight. I'd find something to do at work until half past six. I didn't like coming home. I'd have a bath, have something to eat, then have a bath and go to bed. That was my life for three months. I didn't go out. I pushed all my friends away from me. I wouldn't have my friends round. I just had an awful panic attack one day at work and started to cry and it all came out.

Eileen took some time off work, went to her mother's house to rest, and consulted a good, long-time friend who encouraged her to talk to someone about her rape. When she returned to London, Eileen received a few threatening phone calls from her rapist. Eventually, she moved from her flat and established herself in surroundings where she felt much safer - choosing a place across London, closer to her mother and sharing it with a couple. She also began meeting friends, particularly men, in restaurants and theatres, outside either of their homes, so that she would not be in a situation where she felt vulnerable to attack.

Linda was also raped in her own home, attacked by a man who climbed in through the second-storey window.

I think of my life as pre-rape and post-rape in some ways. I think it altered relationships tremendously. It changed my view of the world and I think it was very difficult with relationships with other women. My best friend and I had a falling out which to this day feels really difficult. I think she was just so totally freaked out by the whole thing. She's a single woman. Suddenly she felt so vulnerable herself. She couldn't deal with it. I was 30 years old, living with my boyfriend, who's now my husband. It was a two-family house. He never went away on business; this night he happened to. We had just moved in about five weeks earlier. I had met a friend for dinner, came home about 8.00. Eventually went to sleep. I do not know whatever time and then around 4.00, 4.15 somebody broke in. He had a knife and threatened to kill me.

Linda was raped. She called the police immediately after he left and reported it. She recalls the police as well-meaning, but incompetent in their handling of her situation. Had she had any other close encounters with sexual assault previously?

When I was in high school we were hitching and there was a bunch of us – about seven of us – and we were picked up by two guys and they took us to some isolated area and said, 'I'm going to rape you.' And I had had a few drinks, but me and another girl were not that drunk but some of them were really drunk. First it was a big joke. And then after a while I and the other woman began to get really scared. Eventually they drove us to a friend's house, but we were really scared. Another time when I was in Germany with a friend we were hitching to Freiberg or something and he took us in the opposite direction from where we were going. We were not going to fall for that. And they threw us out of the car in the mountains, and we were very, very scared. Somebody said Europe was OK to hitch. I've never hitched again in my life.

After the rape, Linda married and moved. She and her husband built the house designed specially for security. She sought safety both in her relationship and in her home. Yet, she still feels more vulnerable at specific times of the year.

I think spring and fall I feel more vulnerable for whatever reason. Fall is the anniversary of the rape. At the park with John [her 2-year-old son], I was very aware that now is the time that people, you know, wear less clothing. Like there's a woman, there's a factory right there so men were sitting there eating, and there's a woman who walked by dressed, you know, high heels, tight jeans and stuff, and I was far enough away that I couldn't hear what they were saying, but just from the body language I could tell. A shudder came through me then. You realise there's no safe place. I think people who can sort of say, 'Well, you know, the deviants out there, you can recognise them, and they have squinty eyes or whatever and it's only .02 of the population who is degenerate.' I think they can operate within a more sense of safety, but I think when you realise it's not those, those are only a very small percentage, you know, your brother, and the man at the corner, and your stepfather, all that. That really changes the perception that indeed you can be safe. There's degrees of safety and circumstances, but . . .

Safety, for Linda, is a continuing process of negotiating potential danger. She is now deeply involved in community groups directed toward combating violence against women. Her experiences fuel her activism which in turn, she hopes, will help her gain control over her own safety.

Women's experiences of rape and attempted rape are all too common. While there are no definitive, aggregate figures, studies of adult women show high rates of sexual assault and rape. Diana Russell's American study of 930 women found nearly one in four experienced a completed rape, and another quarter an attempted rape.[5] Lifetime chances of confronting serious sexual assault, Russell estimates, are a staggering 46 out of 100 women. In a recent survey of college students in the US conducted by *Ms* magazine, one in four young women, whose average age was 21, experienced a rape or attempted rape.[6] No such comprehensive estimates exist in Britain. Clearly, though, the reality of sexual assault is a prime feature of women's understanding of their personal safety.

ON LEARNING SAFETY AND DANGER

Physical Assault

Louise, a native Londoner, lives on what she describes as a 'fairly quiet' estate. She knew about crime because she had been burgled twice prior to moving to her present home. Early one February she was walking home from shopping.

> I had this mugging and it was rather a bad one. I was coming along and I got to the stairs, not these stairs but the stairs you see looking out the window. He just caught me from behind, took the two bags with everything I had in it, shopping and everything and pushed me backwards down eighteen stone stairs. I do not really remember going down them until I hit the bottom. And I did scream out and my neighbour looked out the window and she saw that he was running and they came running out. I had a lump on me head and bruising all along me leg. I just went down backwards. I didn't have any chance to fall right. They said on the report when they did X-ray me was that I didn't have any fractures. I was very badly bruised. I am in terrible pain and I'm in physio[therapy] now. It did shake me up you know inside. I'm just beginning to walk alone home now [ten weeks after the assault]. I did it twice this week. But I am very nervous when I am out. I get these, I do not know, I get these things come over me. Anyone who gets near me are they going to get ahold of me? I seem to be looking around whereas I used to just walk through. I go round the front [of the estate] rather than go around the back.

Before the assault, Louise felt relatively safe on the estate. She would go about her routine with ordinary precaution. For the first ten weeks after the assault, she could not be alone outside her home and felt nervous being inside it on her own as well.

EVERYDAY VIOLENCE

> I work down in the City and I walk there and I do not think of anything. Maybe because there's a lot of people. When you get to your destination, you think 'Oh, God,' and you know you have to walk back here every day.

Louise did not move. She had her husband and daughter walk her to the bus stop in the morning and meet her in the afternoon when she returns from work. Louise is slowly beginning to venture out on her own, still avoiding the staircase where she was assaulted. She mourns the loss of the photographs of her granddaughter in her stolen bag.

Tony, a 42-year-old life-long resident of North London, picked up the company's payroll, walked out of the bank and was accosted by two young men. He ignored their demands for the money, grabbed one and threw him up against a wall. The other sliced his back with a Stanley knife. The wound became seriously infected and Tony was off work for over eight months. A year later, he was still taking anti-depressants and had put his house up for sale, intent on moving his wife and three children to 'safer' surroundings.

> I never really thought about it [my personal safety]. I know I've been robbed. I guess this area was kind of rough. But never have I ever had anything like this happen. You hear about it but you do not think about it. I never used to think anything about going out, whatever time of the night or time of the day either. And the children, we pick them up and drop them off now. There have always been fights and stuff. I've always steered clear of them myself. I know it sounds silly, but I've done karate. I've been a karate instructor, until recently when I had an operation on my legs. I couldn't do much. You could be one of the best fighters in the world so it doesn't matter. It doesn't take but a second. You just forget yourself for a second and that's it. It happens. I had a hold of one of the chaps. And the

other guy came up behind me. And he cut me. He did it so I would let go of his mate. I let go of his mate. I pushed him and he put the thing right down me back. And I thought, 'Oh God, what's he done?' My system went. I just couldn't think. I went numb, completely numb from head to toe. I knew they'd done something sort of bad. I turned round to him and he lunged at me face. I put my arm up and he cut me arm up as well. I mean I had a hold of me chain and he tried to get the chain as well. Pretty soon he's running and the other one is running. Three in the afternoon. I came out of the bank and they just came out of nowhere. I never used to worry about it. Now I go inside the bank and the wife sits out in the car. As long as the car is there I haven't got so far to walk. I've lived here all me life. My sort of teenaged days were when a policeman was stabbed in Seven Sisters Road. It was rough, it was a really rough lot. It was bad then but they never went for normal people. Gang fights. You do not feel as if you can trust anybody [now]. And now when I go out, I can be very wary of anyone coming towards me. Even if it's around the corner to the sweet shop, I go in the car. When I go to the pub when my son plays [in a band], I look for the exits.

Knowledge of karate and an ability to steer clear of danger in the past did not guarantee Tony's safety. His long-term recovery continues to be marred by his overwhelming sense of helplessness, a new and frightening experience for him. He has also focused his anger on black men in general. The intensity of his racism is one mechanism for finding someone to blame for his sudden feelings of vulnerability.

Some young men say that they enjoy a 'good fight'. Frank, a 23-year-old Londoner, describes the experience:

It was actually quite exciting. It was quite exciting to have a fight. It was almost a kind of bonding [between men]. When I look back now, it brought you all together. You joked about it at the pub and didn't think anything of it. It gave you a common goal amongst the group. You were 'all those people from here'. Nobody else could touch you and the feeling of the strength, the security of being within a group. Quite a few [got hurt]. Some good friends – a couple got their arms broken, a couple of them got stabbed. I mean most got hurt at one stage or another.

Surveys always report young men as feeling the safest, yet according to those same surveys they are the most likely to experience physical assault.[7] It is difficult to figure out what percentage of these attacks are the result of fights between friends and acquaintances, as opposed to serious, unprovoked aggression by strangers. The experiences of danger might well vary depending on the man's relationship with his assailant. We do know that women are more likely to be assaulted, both physically and sexually, by male intimates – relatives, acquaintances and friends – than by strangers. Although men are also attacked by men they know, we do not know what effect this has on their relationships with each other.

Fighting back, as Tony did and as Clive also does, is a part of maintaining one's safety. Clive left a club late one evening and witnessed three men savagely beating a teenaged boy. He stepped in when he saw one of them take out a knife.

I come out of a club and there were three men and a young kid, maybe 18, 19. I see these guys with baseball bats, hitting this kid. I noticed the third one had a knife. Then I seen the third one make his way through the other two with the knife. To me, the kid was gonna get badly hurt. They more or less had their backs turned to me. So I had to run in and grab the kid and pull him. As I pulled him the third one hit me with a bat and was holding the knife. He hit me once across the face.

ON LEARNING SAFETY AND DANGER

> Then I was clobbered and clobbered, and more or less held on my knees. They pinned me down and started digging the knife in my head. It was like a frenzy. It is more the way the people done it to me. If it was the case that I had done somebody up a couple of weeks ago, or something like that then I would have to accept it more. The way they done it to me was really vindictive, like I had really done something bad to these people. And they was out to more or less kill me. They had left me for dead.

Clive survived because two men came along, threw him into their car, and rushed him to the hospital. His scars are stark reminders of the attack, as they will cover his face and head forever. Somewhat more philosophical than Tony, Clive just wants to get on with life:

> I try not to let it get in my way. I'm more conscious of things, you know. Transport is my main problem. Travelling on trains bugs me. To get on a train or a bus. I would never think about it before. Now you sort of, I'm more conscious of groups of people on a bus or groups of people on a train. Where before I would get on and I wouldn't bat an eyelid about who was on a train or who wasn't on a train. It's made me very conscious about my safety. Not nervous, but on guard. I noticed it coming back the other evening from over west [London] way. The other night on a train there's nobody on it . . . I know you could be sort of picked out because of the way you dress. You know if you look like a lord gentry office worker type of person you are more likely to get picked on whereas if you are going about in jeans, trainers [tennis shoes] you are less likely to be bothered. Now I know myself if someone got up and said anything I would be pretty good with answers and more or less tell them I know what's going on. I am ready for it whatever comes. He

may think there's me sitting there reading me a book but now I know the score and know everything that's going on around there. It's definitely made me more conscious about what's going on around me. I keep an eye.

Those people who have experiences of extreme violence continue to 'keep an eye'. They step up their vigilance, establish new routines and attempt to find ways to resume their lives.

But for many of us who have not endured life-threatening danger, there are other lessons of unsafety. We may encounter situations that are menacing, but ultimately seem to come to nothing. These, though, are viewed as potentially dangerous and may lead to changing routines for protection. Joyce, a resident of Central Massachusetts, recalls one such experience:

> I was driving to work one night. I had two men follow me in a car on the expressway and the further I would go on the expressway, the closer they would come to me. I could see only their headlights on the passenger side of the car. They wouldn't let me see their licence plate [number]. I kept trying to get off the ramps but they would come close to me so that I could not get off the expressway. Finally I got further on the expressway and I knew something was going to happen to me. I came to a full stop in the middle of the expressway. I waited for cars to pile up, then I gassed it for all it was worth and I got to the bottom of the ramp. I looked up and saw the car and I went into a factory [parking lot]. As I was going into the factory the men in the car came around and drove right through the parking lot. I went in and called my husband. I also called the police department. Now when I'm driving down the road my doors and windows are always locked. I watch who's behind

me and if anyone gets in my way I'll run right over them.

The 'but nothing happened' experiences are, for many, difficult to categorise. There are no injuries, no loss of property, indeed, no signs to others of how serious the threat might have been. Although these events are filed away as knowledge about danger, they may not be shared with anyone else because 'nothing happened'. Yet such close encounters are taken as serious indicators of the potential for violence occurring. Geoff, a 6' 2" actor, recently moved to London.

I was only in London about two weeks when I was sitting down at Waterloo station waiting for a train at 11 o'clock at night. There was nobody else around and I was a little bit on edge about being in London. I've never lived in London before and I didn't know many people. A gang of these skinhead types with the jackets and the boots came down the stairway and along the platform ripping off the vending machine for the chocolate. I could hear glass smashing. They were gradually working their way down towards me and I thought, 'I'm next on the list'. I was just sitting there praying. I was reading my train timetable or trying to. I realised it was upside down. They were getting very close when the train arrived and I jumped into it, in the furthest carriage I could find. Thinking, 'Oh, God, some poor innocent is probably being beaten to death up there, but it's not my business.' And with that the doors open, they were coming through the train! Three of them just came straight over to me and said, 'Right, money.' And just for a second I had enough courage or stupidity just to say, 'No, piss off.' There was just dead silence for a few seconds. I was just waiting. I thought it was gonna be boots and punching and everything else. But one of them said, 'Leave him.' They just passed by me and they went right down the carriage and everybody – old women were opening their handbags and guys were taking money out of their pockets. There hardly seems to be a night when I come home by the tube when something, some sort of a fight doesn't happen somewhere.

Neither Joyce nor Geoff changed their modes of travel. But they do take additional precautions – those they had used had not helped them to avoid confrontation. These varied experiences teach us about potential danger and are a reminder that we too could become victims. That is why, when we hear about others' experiences of violence, we may be listening through an understanding of a near miss of our own. We are alerted to potential danger and motivated to refine or reconsider our routines of safety.

ADULT LESSONS: INDIRECT EXPERIENCES OF VIOLENCE

Hearing about others' close encounters with violence does not automatically give rise to concern for one's own safety. It all depends upon how people understand their vulnerability. One looks at the circumstances, the parties and locations involved and the strategies of protection already in use. We each have such different tolerances and, given our wide range of occupations, living situations and lifestyles, risks obviously vary significantly.

Those who earn their living through the underground, illegal economies consider danger a normal part of their work that they must manage, but can rarely avoid. Drug dealers, prostitutes and back street gamblers, for example, know that their customers, competitors and bosses may use force. People who work in these kinds of jobs are highly likely to have experienced violence and are not surprised by it. While violence may be part of doing business or socialising for some people, most of us learn more about safety and avoidance of danger by being exposed to it through the experience of others.

ON LEARNING SAFETY AND DANGER

Brutality in the home is often hidden and unrecognised. Yet for those who live next door to such violence it can be worrying and distressing. Cynthia, a resident of Central Massachusetts, describes her neighbours:

> There have been three families in a row that the husband beats up on the wife. I could hear every word, every hit, every bounce against the wall because I'm right upstairs from them.

People whose work brings them into contact with those who are victimised in their own homes know that violence is a common occurrence. Margaret, a school counsellor in Massachusetts, notes:

> I see a lot. Maybe it's because the people that are working with special ed[ucation in the US], we see a lot. We begin to see a certain pattern develop and we're apt to say, 'Do you think there's incest involved here?' This is in the last two, three years. All the way down to kindergarten, all the way up to senior high school. I had two kids on my case. They [the molesters] were both church members of the Fundamentalist group. One was a deacon, one was a boy scout leader.

This exposure to violence may help the professionals to come to terms with their own experiences, or guide them in their efforts to protect the safety of others. Kathy explains about her routines of safety:

> A few times, like I used to run [jog] and when I ran at night I really was uncomfortable and I stopped that. I just didn't feel safe doing it. I do not feel I could protect myself. Maybe because I work with victims of domestic violence in my job and I am really aware of rape. It's just because I work with it often and am surrounded by

it or it's happened to me in a past life. I think it's one of
every woman's fear. I really have a fear about that kind
of violation. I'm really conscious about making sure that
if I do go out that I park somewhere safe. I lock my door,
you know.

One lesson learnt by exposure to others' experiences of
violence is the ability to read the signs of danger. Lynn,
a criminal prosecutor in one of the major New England
cities, notes:

As part of that job I know a lot of people, not personally,
and have had contact with a lot of people who have had
their homes broken into. And that's why, like I never
used to lock the window of my fire escape. But I had a
young woman who was asleep in bed who woke up to a
man on top of her and was raped and beaten. He came
in through a window on the fire escape. That always
has just stayed in my mind because of what I learned
in my job. That's why I take that precaution now, after
being educated to that type of crime. I also know of a
friend that was raped. And in her own home. She was
seven months pregnant. She was a single mother and
she was sleeping and an intruder came in the house. I
know her from high school. And she's real close to my
cousin. I know that and I know various people from
work. I deal only in violent crime.

Family or friends are also sources of information about others'
experiences of violence. Cynthia, who earlier reported hearing her male neighbours battering their wives, feels additional
vulnerability through her sister's experience.

My sister was raped down the street a couple of years
ago. She was walking home from work and he grabbed
her and threw her inside his car, drove away to a place
and raped her. He raped her and dropped her off where

ON LEARNING SAFETY AND DANGER

> he had picked her up and took off. After a month she finally told my mother and me. [I feel] a little safe but I'm afraid. Because the people around here are nuts and then after what happened to my sister, I know there are people that come right in here and do things to hurt people.

Margaret also has friends and family who have encountered violence in their lives.

> My son was assaulted. He was probably a junior in high school. But I also know women who have been assaulted – usually by their husbands or boyfriends. There are friends of mine who have told me they've been raped, usually by their fathers. I probably know three or four like that.

Awareness of danger also comes from actually witnessing violence. Peter recalls various incidents:

> I've seen people stabbed and hit with beer bottles, all kinds of things. Most of them bar-room incidents and some domestic things too. Sometimes I wish I didn't grow up with all of this. I know that I'm really good in a stressful situation. I witnessed a murder. When the guy was done killing the person he realised there were two people watching him. He tried to kill the two people who were watching him. It just happened to be me and my best friend. My friend went to have a go after the guy and it took all the strength I had to keep him down. We fell through the doors and as we fell through the doors the guy shot into the bar. I saw the guy run for his car. I ran for my truck and as the guy was driving away, I pulled my gun out from under my seat and fired at his tyres. I was in a nice bar in West Palm Beach. It's not a sleazy area. I went home and put my gun on the table and said, 'Take it, Ma.'

Not everyone's indirect experiences of violence are as graphic. Just being aware that danger exists and that you are a potential target may influence your choice of precautions. Jill, who lives in inner London, states:

> When you realise 16-year-olds are taking heroin and bags are being snatched, and I've heard a few horrid stories of events [I'm wary]. We've never been burgled in the time we've been here, actually. But people in the square get broken into on a fairly regular basis.

Knowing about danger and violence contributes to one's anxiety about becoming a victim. But the worry is not evenly distributed. The most significant difference is that of gender. Women's fears restrict their lives more than they do men's. The next two chapters explore how being female or being male affect one's understanding and experiences of safety.

Chapter five

WOMEN, FEMININITY AND SAFETY

Wherever women are, their peripheral vision monitors the landscape and those around them for potential danger.[1] On the street, we listen for footsteps approaching and avoid looking men in the eyes. At home, women are more likely than men to ask callers to identify themselves before opening the front door and to search for ways to minimise conflict with potentially violent partners. Not only do women incorporate countless avoidance tactics into all aspects of their lives – the very meaning of the word safety differs between the sexes. Women understand it to be both sexual and physical, while men tend to think of their safety as physical.

Women's lives rest upon a continuum of unsafety. This does not mean that all women occupy the same position in relation to safety and violence. Many other features of their lives – such as direct experience, class, race, sexual orientation, or physical abilities – will mean that their circumstances differ. Somehow, though, as all women reach adulthood, they share a common awareness of their particular vulnerability.[2] Learning the strategies for survival is a continuous lesson about what it means to be female.

For the most part, women find that they must constantly negotiate their safety with men – those with whom they live, work and socialise, as well as those they have never met. Because women are likely to be physically smaller than men, as well as emotionally and economically dependent on them, they must bargain safety from a disadvantaged position. As men are likely to be women's intimate companions and their colleagues and bosses at work, the very people women turn for protection are the ones who pose the greatest danger.

Women's heightened level of anxiety is born of an accurate reading of their relationship to safety. It is not a misguided hysteria or paranoia. Women's life experiences – as children, adolescents and adults – are set in a context of everpresent sexual danger. Worry about personal safety is one way women articulate what it means to be female and live, day-in and day-out, in communities where women are targets of sexual violence.

Safety advice offered by police pamphlets, popular books, parental instructions and peers' experiences reinforces women's knowledge about vulnerability, but only their vulnerability to faceless assailants. Told to be on-guard and alert at all times, women's concern about personal danger is constantly directed toward the threat of male strangers. The British Home Office, for example, in its £11,000,000 1988–9 crime prevention campaign, gives special advice to women in order to reduce the risk of their becoming victims of crime. For example:

When at home:
- Have reasonable security against burglars.
- Draw curtains after dark.
- Use only first initials on your door and in the telephone directory.
- If you suspect a break-in when you return home, do not enter the house but go to a neighbour's and phone the police.

Out on foot:
- Avoid short cuts through dimly-lit alleys.
- Walk facing the traffic so that a car cannot pull up behind you unnoticed.

WOMEN, FEMININITY AND SAFETY

- Don't hitch-hike or accept lifts from strangers.
- Cover up expensive-looking jewellery.
- If out late, arrange a lift home.
- If you regularly walk home after dark, consider buying a screech alarm. 'Their piercing noise can frighten off an attacker.'
- If you are carrying a handbag, keep it close to your body. Keep keys separately from your bag, with no identifying address on the keys.
- If a motorist accosts and threatens you, scream and run in the opposite direction the car is facing.
- If you think someone is following you on foot, cross the street – more than once, if necessary, to check your suspicions. If you are still suspicious, run to the nearest place where there are other people. Call the police, but not from a phone box where you might be trapped.
- If you go jogging or cycling, vary your route and time so you can't be attacked. Stick to well-lit roads.
- Self-defence classes can give you greater confidence.

On public transport:
- Try to avoid using isolated bus stops particularly after dark. On a bus, sit near the driver or conductor.
- On a train, sit in a compartment where there are other people, ideally in a compartment which will be near the exit at your destination.

When driving:
- When driving alone, be wary of hitch-hikers. If someone asks for assistance on a quiet road, make sure it is a genuine emergency before you open a window or get out of the car.
- After dark, park in a well-lit, preferably busy area. Look around before you get out.

- When you return to your car, have your key ready and check there is no one in the car.

Although not one of these safety tips explicitly mentions sexual assault, they are clearly directed at women because they are seen to be targets for sexual violence. While giving this kind of advice may seem genuinely helpful, most women incorporated precautions like these (and more) into their everyday routines long ago.

So by the time they have reached adulthood, many women have developed an unconscious alarm system which monitors men's behaviour for possible danger. While each woman will devise her own way of using this information none the less, she knows beforehand that it is *she* who is the cause of men's actions. When danger strikes, it is her behaviour that is scrutinised for its lure to men's physical and sexual aggressions. Women are thus warned about hitch-hiking, accepting lifts from strangers (meaning strange men), walking alone after dark, keeping their curtains drawn, opening doors to strangers, and they are subsequently blamed if they do not follow this advice to the letter.

To understand the context for women's concern for personal safety we must understand the lessons in 'being female' that appear in various forms throughout women's lives. As noted in Chapter 4, the proportion of childhood experiences of sexual danger differs markedly for women and men. With over one third of girls reporting at least one experience of sexual threat, intimidation or assault, a significant minority of adult women's lessons in male intimidation began in childhood. Diana Russell's US study, for example, shows that of the 930 women interviewed, 16% reported at least one experience of incestuous abuse and a further 31% reported at least one of sexual abuse from a non-relative, before the age of 18. Her study shows that 38% of the 930 women interviewed actually encountered some form of sexual danger before they were 18, almost exclusively from men. Only 5% of the cases of incestuous assault, and 4% of extra-familiar sexual abuse were committed by females.[3]

The possible encounter with male intimidation is taken for granted, almost to the extent that the possibility of receiving threats from other females is ignored altogether.

Bullying girls can indeed be distressing and frightening for those at the receiving end. As a friend reported to me, 'My mother warned me about boys while I was growing up, but she forgot to warn me about the girls.' One young teenager in West Sussex, England, wrote how her behaviour changed after she had been confronted by the local bully-girl.

> I don the steel toe-capped DMs [Doctor Martins], the heavy make-up and the black clothing and I try this as my own form of self-defence, hoping that I won't be viewed as easy prey.

Girls who are members of street gangs or who are involved in activities of dubious legality may also get into fights with each other. Usually these revolve around one girl's relationship with another's boyfriend. Such an encounter with violence may frighten the targeted girl into turning to precautionary strategies in order to avoid it happening again. In general, though, girls engage in physical fights less often than boys.

Women's childhood experiences of sexual threats and intimidation, overwhelmingly at the hands of men, teach females special lessons about sexual shame. Linda told of two situations, one involving a male friend of the family for whom she baby-sat, and the other, an acquaintance from her neighbourhood:

> I baby-sat for their child. What would happen is the woman would leave and he worked construction so he would sort of get home at a certain hour. I realised many years later that he knew that I was going to be there. I'd think he'd come home early. Because then I

would say, 'Oh, Tony, you got home early,' you know. And I think he probably did that purposely. I think he had fair control of his own time . . . I think there was a denial point of it. I just couldn't understand what was going on. You know, it started with kissing, and then it progressed and then finally I stopped baby-sitting because I could really see that this was, you know . . . It was just sort of something that happened . . . I think it also took me a long time to realise it was a pattern and it would happen again and that, in fact, it was escalating. But it seemed to be pretty compartmentalised. I didn't sort of, I don't think I did sort of make generalisations about much of anything. It was disturbing while it happened, but it wasn't the kind of thing I think I would have thought about a lot. There was the usual, 'Don't tell anybody,' and 'This is your and my little secret,' you know. And then he used to press money in my hand, too, which I always felt [was] like dirty money. There was just a negative taint to it, but I couldn't quite figure out what it was about. I would avoid him like the plague when his wife and my parents were around. I would just avoid him as much as possible . . . It's funny how things come back [while we are talking]. I remember one time walking across the street and this kid who was, I think at that point he wasn't in my class, but he just reached out and grabbed my crotch and I remember being, in some way, more so than some of the ongoing stuff with this man, I was just so mortified. I remember almost fainting. And I think I was by myself and he was with a friend, and I don't know what it was about. But something about that encounter was just so overwhelming, maybe it was the suddenness of it, the unexpectedness of it. I don't know, but in a lot of ways that, or maybe it was just somebody that was your peer. I was so embarrassed and mortified and overwhelmed. I think I just felt so ashamed.

WOMEN, FEMININITY AND SAFETY

The women whose stories appear here tell about encounters that are memorable, but where 'nothing happened'. What women mean by 'nothing' is that they were not actually accosted, or if accosted, they were not actually raped or beaten. Yet at the time of the incident they thought they would be. The humiliation of being attacked silences women so that they rarely share their worries about preserving their sexual integrity. Laura, now 22, recalls one such occurrence when she was 15 years old.

We were staying with my friend in Washington DC. During the day this girl had a friend who was dating this medical school student who went to [a leading] University. And we thought that was the coolest thing. I mean here we are and this girl's boyfriend was in medical school. Well, she asked us over in the daytime and we were hanging out with the boyfriend and his room-mate. And the girl had to work that night, so the two room-mates said to us, you know, we're having a party tonight. So why don't you come by. Yeah, totally, we're going to go, medical school students! That's cool. We decided that we should show up at like 11.30, you know, fashionably late. We rang the doorbell and there was no one there, no party. And they were like 'Hi, we cancelled the party.' Or the party's us, something like that. I don't remember. We didn't think anything of it. This girl was going out with Bruce, the guy with the moustache. They'd been going out for a while, so we didn't think anything of it. So we got high with them. Then I was in the kitchen talking to this one guy and he leaned over and tried to kiss me when I was going into the refrigerator. I was like, 'What are you doing?' It was so weird. So I walked into the other guy's room, Bruce, and I said, 'You're never going to believe this, but your room-mate just tried to kiss me. That's really strange.' He just got up and locked the door. I didn't really [freak out] until after because there's a good thing about the story. And that is that at the time I didn't get really freaked out. I mean this guy was huge, he was really muscular, he's a lot older than me, and he has me down on the bed, and he's taking all my clothes off, and he has all his clothes off. And he's about to fuck me, and there was little I could do. And he was just about to and he was saying, 'Oh, you want it.' All of a sudden, I said, 'Yeah, I do want it.' I was pretending like I did. And he was about to and I kneed him in the balls so hard. I didn't know where the strength came from. But I was just not going to let this person who is stronger than me . . . I mean I found a place where I could really fuck him up. And he flew off of me. I got my clothes on, ran out the door, and the same thing was happening to my friend, but the guy hadn't gotten that far at all, so I grabbed her. We got into the car and just screamed and cried for an hour. I was really embarrassed for a long time. We really didn't know. Had we asked for it or something? And I felt guilty that I knocked a guy out. So we didn't tell anybody. I think now I just get vibes. I was young and naive, and I was just happy that these medical school students asked me out. It's scary that these men are going to be doctors.

Jill, now 31, reported the following episode with her boyfriend when she was 16.

I had a very stable relationship with one boy from 14 to 17, 18 when he went off to college. But he lived up the road and it was terrific for me. We had this really strong relationship which had its dose of heavy petting. But I was always definite. I was terrified of getting pregnant. I didn't want to go on the pill; an abortion was just sort of beyond the canyon for me. Although we sort of got off to a lot of handsy hands, we never sort of did it. And I remember on holiday in Spain when I was 16 we went for this moonlit swim on the beach. He sort of lost control at one time and he had me on the ground, and was in so to speak. And that was the one time and this was with someone that I felt very, very close to, whom I genuinely loved, but there was this one thing that I was not going to have happen to me at that particular time. That's the only moment that I ever, ever felt scared. I registered the complaint and it actually got through to him and it was all horrible for the next 24 hours and then we were lovey-dovey again after that, and fine.

Both Laura's and Jill's experiences occurred with young men whom they trusted. Although Laura barely knew the men, she thought it would be all right because they were training to be prestigious professionals and she knew one of their girlfriends. Although Jill's relationship resumed its 'lovey-dovey' quality, she none the less remembers this incident as a frightening one. Lynn, now 27, speaking about one occasion on which she had felt pressured to have sexual intercourse, reflected upon how this and other similar instances have affected her behaviour.

It was in a date situation and it was in college. It was someone who I'd been dating for a while, but not steady and it was the first time we were in bed together. I wanted to stop and he didn't. We ended up not stopping. It's not that that experience [changed my behaviour]. I think it's growing up too and not putting myself in that situation any more. You know, where if I'm in bed with someone it's because I want to be in bed with them and not so much, you know, drinking and the whole college scene. I felt some pressure. I dated him [the man who pressured her] for a while and I wasn't a virgin so I didn't have any real philosophical reasons why I didn't go to bed with him. But we started fooling around and one thing led to another. I kind of felt guilty about it. I felt like I put myself in the situation and which I know is a classic victim's response. That's just how I felt. I just take precautions and I don't play unless I want to go the distance.

For many young women, negotiating adolescent heterosexuality is also negotiating sexual safety. How and when to say no or yes, without losing companionship, intimacy and the status involved in coupledom, is learnt from experience.[4] Young women juggle sexuality and safety and, at the same time, keep their eye on their social respectability. A recent American survey of college women reveals that young women's sexual encounters are, too often, coercive. Over one quarter of the 3,187 women reported forced sexual intercourse and over 60% reported experiences of unwanted kissing, fondling or petting. The average age of the women interviewed was only 21.[5] A recent English study of the early sexual experiences of 150 women between 16 and 21 shows how little control they have over sexual encounters.[6] Asking young women to take responsibility for the risk of AIDS, for instance, does not make sense within the current climate of men's control over young women's sexual choices.

In their discussions with me, women revealed a range of sexually frightening incidents, including incestuous experiences with fathers and uncles, encounters with strangers, neighbours, school companions, siblings and family friends. For a variety of reasons – embarrassment, humiliation, self-blame or self-denial – the women had rarely told anyone else about what had happened. They feared negative judgement and public condemnation for their so-called indiscretions. One woman, raped by a boyfriend when she was 16, had only told a few of her close friends. She recalled a particularly painful occasion, sitting around the kitchen table at college, while others recounted amusing stories about their first sexual experiences. Although she laughed along with everyone else, inside she felt the pain of her memories. Her nose had been broken, she had been severely beaten and she was hospitalised after the attack. The assailant had been her boyfriend for a few years prior to the attack. Because she was working away from home, she kept the rape secret from her parents. Even with many of her closest female friends, she never shared the story of her sexual initiation.

While not all women experience such violent sexual assaults, most women admit that they must 'put up' with sexual intimidation from men. Sexual comments on the street or similar intimidation at work is viewed as one of the hazards of being female. There are, of course, many different responses to such harassment.

Maria: Well, here and there, but I don't pay attention to them. I keep walking and it won't bother me. But if it is the night time and I'm walking, sometimes I do pay attention because I don't know if they are going to turn around and stop and get out of the car or whatever. But if I'm with somebody I don't pay any attention to anything. I just keep walking like nothing [happened].

Margaret: I think when I was younger I got very upset. I was embarrassed and probably, as I got older, if I thought that was happening I tried to think, well, it was because we were in a crowded bus or subway or something. Then I would get angry. My feelings changed about it, I think, as the person was doing it.

Cynthia: Sometimes they [sexual comments] make me feel sexy and sometimes they make me feel cheap, depending on how they present the question or whatever they say. They don't really bother me anyway, either I laugh and say thank you and keep walking or turn around and tell them to go to hell or something. It depends on my mood at that time, I guess, what the outcome is.

Judy: When I was younger I felt enormously embarrassed, just like I wanted to die. Oh my God, embarrassed, humiliated. Really humiliated. Now I feel angry. I really do. I just have a 'fuck you' attitude about it. And I have a sense of humour about it too. I haven't been scared by it. There have been times when that was scary. I never knew quite whether people [sic] would . . . I can remember when I used to jog a lot and people [sic] would go by in their car and they'd comment or when I was bicycling. I actually had one person [sic] reach his hand out and whack me on the bottom going by in a car. It hurt too. And I used to be really afraid that people would follow through. Now I rarely have that reaction to it. And I know the difference between scary and not scary places.

While women say they are not always bothered by sexual comments on the street, they do monitor the context within which these take place. After making sure that no danger follows, some women find reassurance that this time, no apparent harm has been done. Others who have encountered such harassment when they are tired, feeling particularly vulnerable, or somehow off guard, find themselves responding to it as if they are personally violated and assaulted.

It is harder to ignore being touched up. Bea recalls a recent incident which occurred just as she was entering a convenience store.

The funny thing was that I was angry at me after [the incident] because I knew there was something odd about the person [sic] coming and so I made a run for it to get into the store and I was running to get into the store. He picked up his feet and came by me just as I got to the door and pinched my ass. And I thought, my God, I can't, you know. I was very, very angry because I knew something was wrong. I should have stayed where I was rather than trying to get in [to the store]. It's like I was figuring out what I could have done differently, you know, what I should have done. And of course I went into the store and certainly wouldn't want to tell anyone in there what happened.

Bea gives us some insight into how self-blame operates to keep women silent about the daily indignities of sexual intimidation. She feels *she* should not have entered the store when she felt something was wrong or perhaps *she* should have known that this man's behaviour was not quite right. Early warning signals, our intuitive sense of vulnerability, do not always shelter women from the 'little rapes'.

While women often define public spaces as potentially dangerous, their frequent experiences of sexual harassment at work indicate that familiar environments are also threatening. Colleagueality, here, is damaging to the health of the woman. The psychological, physical and sexual damage is perhaps diagnosed as undue stress caused by the job, noting symptoms of stress, such as sleeplessness, disruptions in eating habits and irritability. A recent survey of 797 women in England found that one in six women reported at least one incident of sexual harassment in her current job.[7] A US survey of 23,000 federal workers reported that 42% of interviewed women had experienced sexual harassment within the past two years.[8] Such experiences trigger avoidance and precautionary strategies similar to that women use on the street. Women monitor their colleagues' behaviour for danger and threats and may limit their movements to certain parts of the workspace where they feel safer. The search for safety may lead them to search for another job. After such encounters women may fear coming and going to work, as well as feeling more vulnerable to attack.

Some women encounter sexually threatening behaviour from those in positions of authority, such as teachers, police officers, doctors, psychiatrists and lawyers. Sylvia angrily recalled being propositioned by her lawyer during the negotiations of her divorce.

> I didn't tell anybody. I didn't report him. The only witness was the person who went to the lawyer's office with me and viewed my upsetedness when I walked out. He knew something was wrong. It surely added to my cynicism about men and their power. I recall even saying to him, 'What kind of way is this for you to behave?' He had his own sad story. Whatever. Recently married too. I dropped the lawyer.

Margaret, widowed in her 20s with three young children, recalled receiving a number of unwanted sexual propositions after her husband's death.

> One of the things I noticed after I was widowed is that I got a lot of propositions. From the mailman, the rubbish man. I changed him [the rubbish man]. The mailman I couldn't. And then there was an acquaintance who, by way of 'helping' out, made remarks, 'I'll come over and help.' That happened for two or three years, off and on. I'd just come off a situation and that would be it. On the other hand I think in the long run that affects you in your relationships with other people. It keeps you at a distance. You never know who's going to say something.

Being propositioned for Sylvia or Margaret was so sufficiently intimidating that they avoided future encounters with those men and subsequently any other man who might decide that any woman on her own somehow needs sex. Both silently endured unwanted sexual behaviour from publicly respectable men.

Obscene phone calls are the background noise of sexual intimidation for most women in modern life.

> *Maria*: My phone number was private, but I couldn't recognise the voice, who he was. But I knew it was a male, and he knew me and knew what I was going to

do. He knew where the kids' father lived. It was scary. I was so upset I called my mother and she told me to be careful.

Sylvia: I hate them. There's something unreasonable about the fear that it does evoke because when they were coming regularly I started to get real scared because I was alone, but I still had my son in my house. But he was just a little kid in many ways. And I had the glass doors and I was sleeping down here with the glass doors and the fact that the guy used my name made me aware that he knew who I was. And I started thinking, what if this guy has some sort of weird obsession or something. But they stopped. I've never been overly paranoid about them. They're just unpleasant to get.

Judy: A little bit scared. It's really hard not to feel scared. You keep trying to talk yourself into not being scared. It's really hard, especially living alone. And absolutely furious. Really furious that a person was doing that. Scared and furious.

Linda: Well, it's a real invasion, actually. You feel like every time you pick up your phone it could be somebody . . . I've gotten phone calls where they've actually asked for me. Somebody else has picked up the phone, and they ask for me and then it turns into an obscene phone call.

The most worrying aspect of obscene phone calls is that the caller might know you and that a friend, casual acquaintance, lover, or co-worker who treats you normally in public, chooses to intimidate sexually in private. The danger women feel is that somehow the caller will act upon his sexual threats. Linda's rapist followed his attack by phone calls.

After being raped he called back the apartment a number of times. Well, actually, he called upstairs because he had gotten the phone number when he broke into the car and took the woman upstairs' bag or address book, and [then] broke into my apartment, raped me, and then he kept on calling the house but it was the house upstairs because it was her number.

By having a telephone, women are forced to deal with sexual intrusions, potentially each time the telephone rings. When the male caller also has some details about her life, the situation may indeed be very frightening. But to many, receiving an obscene phone call is just one of those things where 'nothing happened'. No one was hurt, no face-to-face confrontation occurred.

Obscene phone calls are so commonplace that the telephone companies have procedures for complaining about 'nuisance' calls. What the phone companies advise the receiver to do is to make note of the time and day of the call. If you should receive more calls from the same caller, and if these calls persist over a repeated period of time, the phone company will advise you to change your telephone number. Telephone companies already advise women not to include their own first names in the telephone book. A woman's name in the phone book, it seems, is a flag for a man who wishes to make obscene phone calls. Our connection to the modern world, the telephone, is commonsensically understood as a tool for sexual intimidation.[9]

Sexual safety is so fragile for women it can be shattered each time the media spotlight a tragedy of random violence against women. We are constantly surrounded by daily news stories of other women's misfortunes. In one particularly harrowing case in England in 1988, a woman's car broke down on the highway on an early summer's evening and she went to call the police for assistance. She left her sister and 18-month-old child in the car, walked half a mile to the phone, and disappeared. She was found dead three days later. Women who read about this seemingly ordinary situation turned into lethal danger rightly understand that they too could be the target of wanton violence.

News travels fast about the 'local rapist' or a set of unexplained killings of women. Women become more vigilant during times of such threats. When my neighbourhood in the US was targeted by a 'local rapist' (this happened twice in five years in a small city), my own anxiety rose. During these episodes, I altered some of my daily routines. For example, one rapist crept up back stairwells and somehow entered women's locked apartments. For a few months, I did not use the back entrance to my house. I put new locks on both the front and back doors. I used the university escort service to take me home after my evening classes. And when the rapist disappeared – he just stopped and was never caught – I slowly eased back into my old habits. I no longer felt it necessary to maintain that level of vigilance. But some features of my safety procedures permanently changed. The locks are different and more effective. I enter my house using the front entrance rather than the back. The acute level of anxiety has waned, but the legacy of precaution remains. While caution is part of most women's everyday behaviour, there are those who forcefully remark that they will not be restricted by fear of sexual attack, nor let it interfere with their lifestyles. When I ask about whether they take ordinary measures for safety, such as monitoring their surroundings, they admit that they do take precautions, but claim that it does not restrict their lives. Clearly, for a significant proportion of women, self-confinement is seen as a solution to the fear of public places at night. Margaret Gordon and Stephanie Riger, authors of *The Female Fear*, interviewed 299 US women about their use of precautionary strategies. Forty-two per cent stated they used isolation 'staying at home' 'all or most of the time' or 'fairly often'.[10]

Many women turn to men – their companions, sons, or friends – for protection. Jane, who has a keen awareness of the dangers of New York City, states, 'I feel safer when [my husband] is with me as opposed to me being by myself.' This feeling, echoed by many other women, is that men provide defence against outside danger. Some women who live with men report changing their behaviour inside the house when the man is away, sleeping in different rooms or over at a friend's house, or perhaps asking someone to come and stay for the duration of the man's absence. Other women leave additional lights on. When my partner is away, I have the cats sleep in the room, so that if they hear any movement downstairs, they will jump up and run toward the noise (forever in search of additional food, these cats). Yet I feel better knowing that I will have advance warning of any intrusion.

Women who live alone are recipients of special advice on how to protect themselves. The assumption is that individual men will protect individual women from the dangers of other men. This assumption overlooks the fact that, if women are in danger, it is far more often from the hands of their 'protectors'. Moreover, even with the best of intentions, women's 'protectors' are not present 24 hours each day. Women not only become their own defenders, for themselves and their children, but also they become the agents of their own internal controls, in order to avoid danger. What happens, though, when all of women's efforts do not protect them from harm? While many women may anticipate danger, what changes occur after a woman has experienced violence? How does this affect women's feelings about their safety?

Zoe, a 33-year-old accountant in London, observed all the rules. She lives alone and is an accomplished businesswoman.

> I've always been fairly brave, some call it stupid. I've always been aware of someone walking behind you, or groups of youths, black and white. I'd cross over to the other side of the road [to avoid them]. Only a few people close to me have had anything happen. I always took my key out of my bag and put it in my pocket just

in case. I always wondered how I'd get on [if something happened]. Would I kick or scream? As soon as I saw him I just knew. I kept on hoping it wouldn't happen. I looked over my shoulder and heard a rustling and he was coming up behind me. I held my hand-bag close. Next time I turned round he was right behind me. I cowered away from him. I was immediately angry. I started running after him. I screamed something out. And I just walked home. I still feel relatively safe in my own road. What I do now is that I get a taxi from the train stop to the door because I can't get myself to walk down that road.

Zoe's confidence was shattered for a few months after her bag was taken. She suddenly felt acutely vulnerable to attack, found sleeping almost impossible, avoided friends and generally went through a stressful time, virtually unable to concentrate at work with such a severe lack of sleep. It was hard for her to explain why she felt so devastated by having her bag snatched. She was not hurt, she did not lose a lot of money, although the inconvenience of cancelling credit cards and renewing her drivers' licence reminded Zoe of the incident. Having taken the usual precaution of putting her keys in her pocket, she was able to go home and call the police. Having her bag snatched taught Zoe that no matter how cautious and in control she was, she could be vulnerable. That lesson brought on depression and anger.

If I am going out with a friend, they have to meet me. If someone is around me, I am nervous. It's not stopping me from going out, but I have to make plans about getting back. I am aware of all the possibilities. I don't trust anybody. I have cut down a lot [on what I carry]. If my bag is snatched again, I won't have as much to lose. They get my umbrella and a plastic bag. I see women now with handbags and I feel like warning them.

As time went on, Zoe's anxiety lessened, but her new awareness was incorporated into her understanding of her own vulnerability. 'It's the price you have to pay, especially if you are a woman. It makes me annoyed.'

While having one's bag snatched or being burgled is generally not considered sexually threatening, women often feel as if they were or could have been in such danger. Experiences of other forms of crime or nuisances may be felt more deeply by women, particularly those who are survivors of sexual assaults. In speaking to such women, I found that they are likely to use a variety of precautionary strategies, heightened when confronted by a particular danger or type of danger that reminds them of that previous attack. Women who have been raped, for instance, typically develop a series of exaggerated avoidance tactics, at least in the period immediately following the assault. After an experience of such an intimate intrusion, many women find it difficult ever to feel safe. Eileen, who was raped by an acquaintance in her flat (see Chapter 4, pp.68-70), avoided the lounge for three months, and took at least three baths a day, sometimes using bleach, in an attempt to feel clean.

> I was getting very panicky. I'd be at my desk at work and I couldn't bear to be there. I wanted to be doing something else. I had to get out of the building. I'd have to go out and walk. You can't do that too often without people noticing . . . So I decided that I wanted to move. This place came up. It was with a couple. I would never have gone and shared with a bloke. At the moment I wouldn't. It seemed a bit safer, being with a couple, the flat was where I wanted it, it was the first place I saw, and I just wanted to get out. I haven't got the capacity for stress that I tended to have, I get upset a lot more easily over very silly things that never would have bothered me before. That's dependent on the mood of the day, really. I'm very moody from it all, I must admit.

After receiving threatening phone calls from the rapist at her former flat, Eileen finds ways to safeguard herself from the possibility that he can locate her.

> I do have a telephone now, but it's not in my name. If it's listed, it is listed in the landlord's name. It certainly would not be listed in mine. And all my phone calls at work are screened. All my phone calls at work go by my secretary, so I don't get any direct calls.

Eileen did not report the rape initially, but eventually informed the police because of the rapist's threats. She moved, leaving behind the physical reminder of her assault. A year later the acute anxiety and fear has now waned, though periodically she feels acutely vulnerable to sexual assault, especially when the news carries reports of another serious assault on a woman.

Many women come to fear the men with whom they live. Women who – at least from an outsider's viewpoint – have supposedly safe, ordinary existences also know danger. They may live in the suburbs, work only at home and be married to apparently solid, presumably safe, members of the community. Periodically, they may fear their husbands' tempers, or are subjected to beatings. A small proportion of women face lethal brutality from husbands, ex-husbands, or current and past boyfriends. One in three women killed in Britain is murdered by a husband, lover or former intimate.[11] More commonly, women experience violence and intimidation from partners, ranging from verbal abuse to constant beating. Many who fear their partners leave before things get worse. (See Sylvia's account, Chapter 2, p. 31). Bea, divorced from the man who was violent, describes his intimidation of her:

> We were married eight years. This is very hard to explain. It sounds bizarre. I would say in those eight years there were probably eight times. It was almost

like a once a year – looking back on it, I'd say perhaps he didn't know how to deal with the little things that I did that irritated him. So that he could, I'm only guessing, let them mount up and then once a year lose complete . . . because whenever he would lose control, it would be something completely absurd. Or that you knew, obviously, that that wasn't the thing that made him angry. The interesting thing is that he wanted a divorce. I always think of that. Had he not wanted a divorce, I might still be in that relationship. Some of the things that frighten me because I was hurt that he wanted a divorce. Today I'm so happy that it happened but . . . No, he didn't beat me. I always say that, even when we went to court. He would just grab me by the neck and throw me. And that would be the end of it, so I always felt like that's not too much to put up with . . . Mom had already told us that you don't tell anybody. I had filed for divorce when I finally shared it with my sister. I feel for myself personally that I'm a very fortunate person. I don't know how to explain it. I became very determined at that point in my life that that was it. That nobody ever, ever again. I got into a relationship with a man right after that divorce. Fortunately that man was probably 5' 5", did not weigh much more than me, and on one occasion I can remember him kind of hinting that maybe he was going to attempt to knock me around. I remember telling him that I might, I might be able to take him. And it never happened. And I also remember when my current husband and I seemed to be heading toward talking about marriage, I remember saying 'If you ever, ever, ever touch me and I will call the police.' I've never known if this man would have thought on these lines you know.

Because many women struggle to keep relationships together, even in the face of violence, they are often accused of enjoying it or, in some cases, asking for it. Women may even find a reason to justify their husband's actions, like Bea above. She attributes her husband's behaviour to his irritation at her. We do not know how many women are willing to trade being grabbed around the neck and thrown to the ground once a year if her relationship and the financial, social and emotional ties remain intact.

Just as some women manage unpredictable violence at home, a small proportion of women live within violent worlds, like women who work as street hustlers. These women also find ways to live with the daily threat of danger, even from the men they live with. Eleanor Miller, author of *Street Woman*, suggests an explanation,[12] one that does not sound too different from the reasons why women might stay with threatening and violent partners.

> Women on the street have no status without a 'man' to party with, 'love', provide one with drugs and offer protection. The women will say that they need a 'man' for protection. In fact these 'men' offer little by way of protection and are themselves the primary threat to personal safety. They say they need them to prevent other predatory 'men' from using force to recruit them to work for them. In fact, there are strong norms against 'men' stealing women from one another, although they try. They have to make it seem that the women freely choose them. The Catch 22, then, is that women really carry the burden of their own control. If approached by another 'man', it is their job to make the 'man' leave them alone. If it looks like they are at all friendly or engaging in flirting behaviour, the 'man' they work for will beat them. Thus, women cannot freely look for the best working conditions. At the same time, women feel that if their 'men' did not react in this way it would mean that they did not care for them; 'good "men"' are supposed to act jealous and beat them as a result of that jealousy. Female street hustlers feel that they need to be

kept in line by these men or else they would act in ways dangerous to themselves and others.

We may believe that women who work the street are very different from all women. But they are not. Women in general are also 'kept in line' by their fear of danger, a climate of sexual intimidation, and public condemnation for women who do not follow the rules of safety.

We are nowadays more aware of the potential for sexual violence in courtship and dating, as such incidences are being reported more frequently. And as we begin to understand the use of coercive sexuality and rape in marriage, so we must acknowledge that sexual violence is not solely a problem from strange men – it is a very component of women's relationships with all men.

Chapter six
MEN, MASCULINITY AND SAFETY

For men, there are no tips about personal safety in crime prevention handbooks. It is assumed that men either know about avoiding dimly-lit alley ways and bus stops, or that they are able to protect themselves. While we may assume men already know how to protect themselves, they don't seem to be very successful: men's recorded levels of victimisation are much higher than women's.

Yet most men, according to crime surveys, report feeling safe enough to venture on to the streets alone after dark.[1] When asked if they are concerned about crime, men usually respond that they are not worried about their own safety, but about that of others. This apparent altruism focuses on their mothers, wives or children.[2] When men do worry about crime, it is about their property rather than their persons.[3]

Men manage danger quite differently to women. When men do express concern about safety, it is largely an unease about physical safety, their wariness directed toward groups of young men. While many men admit using precautionary strategies, these are often employed only in particular situations or places. Men who wish to avoid violence simply keep away from a particular pub or bar, football match or area of the city where they feel danger lurks. Unlike women, men seldom feel the need to isolate themselves in their homes in order to avoid potential danger.

EVERYDAY VIOLENCE

Men learn to negotiate physical danger, largely in the company of other men. Safety comes from strength, backed up by physical ability and enhanced by the advantages of economic, racial or sexual status. A 'real' man is a strong, heterosexual male protector, capable of taking care of himself and, if necessary, guarding his and others' safety aggressively. He is the man who will stand up in a fight, but will not abuse his power by unnecessarily victimising others. And, according to the mythology of the 'real man', he will do so fearlessly.

Men, like women, accumulate experience about personal safety throughout their lifetimes. Lessons learnt in childhood, adolescence and adulthood teach men when to keep their distance from fights, to stand their ground when threatened, or to initiate aggression as a way of protecting or establishing, as Gordon states, in Chapter 2, 'Who's better than who, who's bigger than who, who's stronger than who.' Clearly, young adult experiences do not entirely determine how men will tackle the world when grown. But most men, according to crime surveys, say they feel relatively safe. How have they managed to get themselves into such a position? Is this merely because, as men, they cannot admit to fear because being afraid is an affront to masculinity? Does being male account for why most men say they feel relatively secure from violence, despite evidence of their recorded encounters with sub-lethal and lethal violence?

GROWING UP: BARGAINING WITH MASCULINITY

Vic Seidler suggests that, 'as boys, we have to be constantly on the alert to either confront or avoid physical violence. We have to be alert to defend ourselves . . . Masculinity is never something we can feel at ease with. It is always something we have to be ready to prove and defend.'[4] No doubt, learning how to manage other boys' violence is a key lesson when growing up male. 'Yeah,' replied Stan, a 37-year-old electrical mechanic from Massachusetts, 'I think we all [his male friends] went through a fight at one time.'

Most men I interviewed recalled incidents of fighting while growing up. Their stories, however, varied a great deal. Not all physical confrontations were the 'usual' events such as those described by Kevin, a 32-year-old Massachusetts security officer, as the 'same amount of fights as any other 13- or 14-year-old kid.' Some boys were clearly victims, others, victimisers. Many, at some point, used fights to resolve arguments, to establish territory, or to display the fact they were 'real' men and a few succeeded in steering clear of physical altercations altogether.

Many adults condone and reinforce the use of physical power by boys as proof that the child will grow up to be a 'real man'. Tom Ryan, a psychotherapist, finds that men's concerns with masculinity are tied to their need to prove their masculinity.[5] One client, Dave, recalled having to answer to his brother or father if he avoided a fight. They would demand that he schedule rematches if he retreated from battles with other boys, in order to teach him to stand up to a fight. Gordon, who grew up in suburban New York, knew that his childhood and teenaged skirmishes established some kind of pecking order in the neighbourhood. Unlike Kevin, who feels that men's teenaged struggles over esteem and power are natural states of affairs, Gordon reflects upon the impact of his encounters with violence.

> If you took the same instances [of violence] and applied it to adults, it would be considered crime, you know. People turn around and say, 'This is kids.' We're just growing up. Yeah, I would say it's a crime because I've seen [violence], I've experienced [it], I know what kids are like.

Throughout, men's biographies and early self-awareness about violence reflect a dynamic and subjective understanding of masculinity as a site for power struggles.

Boys' physical confrontations are typically considered normal by those who believe that participating in fights toughens boys and shows them how to be men. Robert, raised in New York City housing projects, recalled, 'Well, there was always the kids that would try to get your milk-money when you were a kid . . . Then in junior high [school] they're into tougher stuff.' In order to survive one learns to manage the milk money shakedowns, then learns to manoeuvre through more serious physical confrontations.

While most fighting amongst boys is considered 'natural', some take the brunt more than others. Fred, now living in Central Massachusetts, grew up in a small town and felt he was continuously victimised because the other boys did not consider him to be a 'real man' because he is gay:

> We moved to a mill town outside of [a Connecticut city when I was 6]. I was constantly getting beat up by the other kids. It was constant terror . . . I can't recall a specific situation. I can recall a series of situations and people that beat me up. But I didn't like to remember them . . . It was kids around the neighbourhood assaulting me constantly . . . Then, when I went to high school, which was a new nightmare, it was essentially a lot of the guys, the 'real guys', that were the . . . I mean, I was afraid to go to the bathroom . . . At 13, I think I was the only communist at [high school], and I was getting beat up for that too. I thought that went out a long time ago [during the McCarthy era]. I wasn't in high school that long ago. [Fred is 27 years old.] I used to get beaten up for being a fag. I used to get beaten up for getting As [good marks in school]. So I was a target. Even the night of my senior dinner [just before graduation from high school], I guess I was still 17, I was in the bathroom and I was beaten up by ten guys. They stopped beating me up eventually because I threw up on their shoes. All the teachers that were there knew what happened.

> The only thing that any one of them did was come up to me and say, 'For a faggot, you're not that bad of a person.'

Fred stepped outside what was considered to be acceptable behaviour and was punished by fellow students and teachers. Young men learn about the unspoken rules dictating proper masculine behaviour. Advocating alternative, supposedly 'outlandish' political beliefs, achieving academic success amongst educational mediocrity or choosing men as sexual partners each violates what is 'normal' for young American men. Fred knew he was a target for the hatred and intolerance of those around him. He also knew those in authority would not protect his freedom of speech or admire his scholarly ability. Nor did his teachers intervene to stop the abuse Fred received for being homosexual.

Boys and young men like Fred are likely to be punished for not being heterosexual. It seems that part of learning to be masculine also means learning to choose women as sexual partners or at least as the objects of sexual interest. Heckling or sexually harassing women is a form of sport for groups of young men. Keeping men heterosexual ensures that men retain their position of dominance *vis-à-vis* women, and this dominance is considered a natural extension of how women and men relate to each other. By demanding that men be heterosexual, other boys and men carve out a proper place amongst men.

Young men who are heterosexual or apparently heterosexual display intense hostility towards homosexuals and homosexuality in language and deeds. Gary Alan Fine, in his study of pre-adolescent boys' little-league baseball teams in the US, found the common use of name-calling which served to feminise boys who were not 'acting' appropriately male.[6] 'Sissy', 'faggot', or 'queer' are only a few of the terms that boys use to denigrate and humiliate each other. By 'feminising' some boys, others can boost their own self-image as 'true' men.

Negotiating heterosexuality involves sorting out the hierarchies and the power relations amongst 'real' men. This process of negotiation has one advantage for many, but not all, men. It guarantees that most sexual violence is directed toward women. By separating themselves from homosexuals and homosexualiy, many young men feel they can separate themselves from sexual danger. Unlike women who largely experience sexual danger from the opposite sex, men view homosexuals as constituting potential sexual danger. Only one man, Mike, reported experiencing sexual danger from an adult man.

> Those were confusing and scary [experiences]. I remember one time [I must have been] 12. It was just one person, a couple of different instances. It was in this park, not well-lit in the downtown area . . . A man grabbed me in the genitals . . . Well, I just started staying really away from the park and I think that being scared of gay men, or men who look like they may be gay or look like they may look at my body.

David Finkelhor's US research estimates that approximately one in eleven boys experienced some form of sexual threat or abuse.[7] The studies of adult sexual offenders show that males who victimise boys are more likely to consider themselves heterosexual than homosexual.[8] One acquaintance of mine, for instance, was sexually abused by a friend of his family. The man, married and living with his wife, approached my friend during the night while his wife was sleeping upstairs. Hostility and blame for the sexual abuse of male children is focused on homosexuals. While girls are still more likely to be abused by adult male heterosexuals, boys are also targets.

Another mechanism for denigrating other men and justifying violence is racism. Ricardo recalls being beaten when he was 11 years old, on arrival in Massachusetts, because he was Puerto Rican:

> I join[ed] a gang, [and] that is something that I'm not that proud of because I did things that I didn't want to. You had to do them or else you get beat up yourself. So you do it or they'll do it to you. I had a little gang myself at one time. It was to protect each other due to the fact that it was a racial thing going on and we used to fight whites, blacks and anyone that used to get in our way. We used to protect each other in our neighbourhood, at school, anywhere. And one time, one of my friends got beat up and he came to us and told us and in return we sent two of those guys to the hospital, brutally beaten up because he was our friend. They beat him up just because he was Puerto Rican. It wasn't because he did something wrong to them.

Threatening, intimidating or assaulting someone because he is a particular race or a member of a religious group imposes an order into men's relationships with each other. Pete, who grew up in the same town as Ricardo, also recalls fights between racial groups (see also page 60).

> There were small gang fights here and there, but they didn't amount to anything. They were racial, between blacks and Puerto Ricans. The cops would pull up and see us all with baseball bats and beers, and they'd say, 'Keep it clean,' and drive away. When they said, 'Keep it clean,' they meant no knives, that's all.

Fine's study of boys' little-league baseball teams did not uncover a large number of physical fights among male pre-adolescents in the suburbs. Whether fighting is universally common to males – and Seidler earlier suggests that at least the avoidance of it is common – many of the men in this study could assess their ability to stand up to a fight along a continuum of possible physical confrontations they might encounter. The judgements are linked to their experiences or those of their friends, not to a universal understanding of their vulnerability to violence because they are male. Moreover, the men made distinctions between what is a fair fight – a confrontation between two boys with more or less the same skills – and an unfair fight – one where one side is outnumbered or when weapons are used against the unarmed.

Some young men sought additional training in self-defence. Boxing, weight-lifting and instruction in the martial arts are just three avenues men choose to improve their physiques and their physical ability. Although participation in such rigours may increase a young man's confidence to defend himself, it may cause other problems. A large or obviously strong man may become a target for those who feel that, if they fight and defeat him, they will gain greater esteem. Stan states:

> I never considered lifting weights or anything like that. I took some boxing. I never considered that for fighting. I mean I used it in my fighting, obviously . . .

Other men choose to participate in sports such as football to keep fit. To many men, sporting ability underscores how they feel about themselves as men. Mike speculates:

> It's like, I think, a lot of men [if they] really felt how scared they were, they wouldn't have those type of demands, but since you're taught to not show [weakness but] to take pain. That was the big thing when we were playing sports. Playing hockey you learnt to take a lot of bruises and after a while it doesn't bother you. I'll have black and blue marks but I don't remember how it happened. It's like you sort of toughen up. That [the sport] sort of toughens you up so you don't feel the hurt as much when it does happen.

To what extent sports participation contributes to young men's lessons in aggressive competition and legitimate outlets for some outbursts of violence is beyond the scope of this book, though Mike suggests:

> I used to fight a lot with my brothers and occasionally with strangers I would get into fights. [I went into the seminary for high school.] Sports was a real saving grace for me because I had some physical ability and that was where I could hold my own. In the seminary it was in sports that I was able to . . . there was less conflict with others and a more real determination to kind of prove myself but I didn't do that through fighting.

He continues with an observation about risk-taking and masculinity:

> We do a lot of things [as boys] that are really terrifying, and that it was just part of the way you tested yourself. I remember the bridges that go over the railroad tracks and there's a large beam that goes from one end to another. It's like [crossing] an 'I' beam, and we'd crawl all the way across, and it's really terrifying stuff, but [we'd] set up these kinds [of tests] with chums, of climbing really tall trees to the top and if you did you had a sort of exhilaration about it.

This buoyancy, Mike feels, is not without a later price.

> I notice that young boys are really alive, their faces and their attention is really out. I work with a lot of teenagers and you know they've got the really depressed look on their faces. You know, really shot down, and part of that I think is that they're copying the adults. Part of that is the oppression had been laid in for so long and the other is just the real despair about not getting your real needs met and so acting in a lot of angry ways. I remember doing lots of things. Especially

when I was drinking. Stupid. Just vandalism for the hell of it, not even thinking about how it would affect other people or how other people would think about it. Or just destroying other people's property. Not even thinking about these kinds of issues, but generally I would say that was the horrible time of my life. But because I think you can't show how you're feeling, you show it less and less and, the less you show it, the more they [aggressors] think you can take it, so the more they give.

So while some boys learn to confront aggression, other boys also discover how to avoid physical confrontations. Some leave a situation before the argument gets 'too hot', others acquire skills which can help them diffuse tension – the good talkers, still others develop the knack of spotting trouble and so steer clear of it. Choosing friends who do not participate in violence may also reduce the risk of encountering trouble.

A few men admitted that as teenagers they took part in the 'excitement' of the fight. Some looked forward to Friday evening, described as 'pub and a fight' night by Frank. He was 23 at the time of interview and lived in London. He reflects:

When I got to maybe 11, 12, 13, I started getting into the, not gang, but I was in a group of friends and I suppose, you know, from outside we could have been considered a gang. Quite a tough area round here, not as tough as New York, but it's quite tough. And you get into a lot of skirmishes. It's kind of well, like the only way working-class people tend to get respect is – working-class men anyway – is by violence, or being able to beat someone up, or make someone laugh, or having lots of money. Those are the three things that you get respect. So living in a working-class community you tend to kinda conform to those ideas, especially if you're young. You haven't got the strength to stand on your own yet. I mean I was involved in that sort of thing. There was quite a few skirmishes from about the age of say, 13 to about the age of 17. It was actually quite exciting.

One early fight stands out as an initiation into the hazards of pub violence, seen by Frank as providing him with a symbol of bravado – a scar.

> I lost a bit of an ear. I was in a pub with me girlfriend at the time and I went up to the bar. There was a scuffle broke out and everybody stepped back. There was these guys, they were all junkies, you know what I mean, I'm sure of it. They was about 30 but bad people, but junkies. I was 16, half their age. They actually threw these tables up in the air. I didn't step back. I stood there. A little bit of bravado. I didn't expect [to be involved]. I thought, 'I don't know these people,' this can't be nothing to do with me. They obviously took it as a sign. Everyone stepped back now, except me. I'm suddenly in the middle of the pub, on me own, standing there like that, and anyway one of them broke a glass. One hit me over the head with a glass, above me eye, and one hit the back of that [ear]. That was only my first experience, you see, and I got cut in the back of me head as well. I was taken to hospital . . . I always feel that if you live that sort of life and you go to them sort of places where that sort of thing happens then its bound to happen to you eventually. I remember being 16 and it was almost a status symbol. It was almost some kind of a symbol: 'tough geezer, got a scar', you know. I remember thinking that. And I remember loads of people used to maybe think I got sliced with a knife or something and they walk in and it was like, 'All right?' 'Yeah, I got cut last night.' It was almost 'Look, must be a right tough nut,' so I remember thinking that. Then

you get older and you move out and you realise the futility of it all.

The intensity of using violence as one form of achieving respect is heightened for boys who spend time in reform schools or borstal. (The effects of adult imprisonment are described later.) Leo, sent to reform school as a boy of 14, handled his fear of violence by learning to be violent himself.

> It was almost expected that you would have to go into the bathroom area and fight with somebody. And if you didn't then it was just, your locker was cleaned of what little property you had, and you became sexually abused and the works.

Sexual abuse came, said Leo, from both staff and fellow inmates. Leo's own abusive behaviour toward women, he readily admits, was encouraged and taught during his years of confinement. Now 48, he has spent all but approximately four years since the age of 14 in prison. Whatever time he had outside such confinement was laced with aggression and sexual violence.

Most men recalled that it was in familiar settings, such as their schools or neighbourhoods and especially places where boys gathered together, where violence occurred. As teenagers approach adulthood, many outgrow their aggressive stances, but take the knowledge about men's potential violence with them. Frank suggests:

> By [17] I'd moved out of the violence [and so have my friends] . . . We've grown up [together] since we were little kids. And a lot of them, what they did [the fighting and so forth] they grew out of as well, and the ones who didn't, parted company with us. We became a group of friends now, rather than a gang. We don't get into fights and that. We hate it . . . actually fighting disgusts us . . . A lot of them are into making money and that.

MEN, MASCULINITY AND SAFETY

While many boys mature out of their public pursuit of brutality, indeed the peak age for offending the law is between 15 and 25, no one knows how many men are violent within their private relationships, particularly with women. We know from women's experiences that many men are violent and threatening even though, to outsiders, they may enjoy the reputation as a gentle man. Some of these men may have been violent as adolescents, others not. Most men, though, seem to be adept at avoiding violence from other men by the time they reach adulthood.

As men become trained, skilled and educated they may encounter another form of violence from other men. For the new recruits, initiation ceremonies, in fraternities or the army for example, are commonly terrifying. These incidents tend to be regarded as 'good fun' despite the genuine danger and distress involved. One 16-year-old man, living in the North of England, reported an occasion where he was tied up and three workmates poured glue and iron filings on his testicles. Another young man, also 16, was learning the car repair trade. His colleagues and supervisors 'ripped open my overalls and sprayed my balls with paint'. Such episodes, considered harmless by the perpetrators, are those in which sexual degradation is used to assert dominance in the workplace. Yet they are not regarded as posing sexual danger, but as 'unofficial training given by fellow workmates'. The company director, in responding to a letter of complaint by the family of the man sprayed with paint, stated: 'Your letter brought a smile to my face having experienced a similar situation to that of your son when I was an apprentice . . . I am sorry you do not see the funny side of these events.'

TAKING SAFETY FOR GRANTED

Margaret Gordon and Stephanie Riger, studying the fear of crime in three US cities, find that men's management of the possibility of personal violence contrasts sharply with that of women.[9] While 42% of women said that they avoided risks by isolating themselves from them, 90% of men living in the same neighbourhoods reported they 'never bother avoiding such exposure' to dangerous situations. Crime surveys reveal that men's fears for their personal safety are at levels less than one third those of women. In the 1984 British Crime survey, for example, only 13% of interviewed men said they felt 'a bit or very unsafe', where 48% of women revealed they did so when walking alone after dark.[10] It may be that women's as well as men's assessments of safety lie in their assessment of sexual danger. And because men are not subjected to the day-in and day-out sexual intrusion so common in women's lives, they are able to report feeling largely secure.

It seems that many adult men, despite varied histories of involvement in physical violence as children or adolescents, do not regularly restrict their activities, nor do they actively monitor their landscapes for danger with the same vigilance as women do, unless they have been seriously harmed by physical violence. Stan, in discussing his neighbourhood, states, 'I feel very safe.' When asked if he could recall any particular situation where he felt unsafe, alone at night after dark, he gave the following example.

> I think once, the cat had gotten lost and the kids pestered me to go look for it. There's a park by the house and it's like a couple of streets over. I went through there at night and I scared off a bunch of kids drinking, and it [the fear] was a couple of seconds of [thinking], you know, what's going to happen? But other than that, I've been in worse situations so I don't worry about those. [Stan is a veteran of the Vietnam war.] I don't have a problem in a lot of instances with that. My wife does. Like I said, there's these families with loud people that live in there. We're both very quiet people. So she feels unsafe at night. She [yells to me], 'I'm going to take the clothes off the line, listen for me,' you know. That's our routine.

Mike, too, compared his own feelings about his neighbourhood with those of women. When asked how safe he feels his neighbourhood to be, he replied, 'It's safer than some but yet it's not one in which women walk alone in at night.' Earlier, he was asked about whether he could describe how he regularly walked down a street – a question many women answer in great detail. He stated:

> What makes it hard, in talking about men in general, [is] the tendency to having been conditioned to [block feelings] out so that you don't feel the fear, or you can't say, 'Well, what's happening right now is fear.' It's just like we've been so numb to our feelings that we're not really conscious that that's what we would be feeling – fear – at the time. And so if somebody said, well, you're feeling scared, it's like [you say] you're wrong. I'm not feeling scared. It's simply because I'm numb to the feelings that we do have. I remember having some sort of a caution about going to the store [in a dangerous area] and being cautious, and having some sense of how I'd respond to a situation of being assaulted. I think the fact that I know that they wouldn't want to rape me was kind of a thing where I'm more concerned with my money than anything else. That was pretty much of an issue. So if that's what they wanted, that'd be real easy for me to do. I knew that. I have no problem parting with my money, especially with the money I did have. So for me, I wouldn't have put up a resistance. I would either try to connect with them [to try and talk them out of it] or if I was too terrified to do that, just go ahead and give them my money and not resist. There was never the other factor – being raped. I don't think I ever thought that could happen to me. The only time that I ever feared being raped would be if I ever went to jail.

Men name prison as the place where they say they would fear sexual violence. The studies of such assault in prison show that rape is, in fact, a rarity there. Sexual exploitation and coercion is far more common. The process of sexual exploitation, in and outside of prison, is one that serves to enhance heterosexual masculinity. Inmate power and control can be gained by treating other inmates 'like women', essentially keeping the fear of sexual danger associated with being female. By turning some men into 'women', these inmates use sexuality to dehumanise and degrade fellow inmates. To safeguard an inmate's manhood and manliness, an inmate must fend off sexual attacks and be wary of sexual approaches.[11] One man, who was raped in prison, stated:

> I am thinking: What would a real man do in situations like this [rape]? . . . Well I was upset because first of all, most guys consider themselves a man, and you always say that in jail no one is ever going to do that to you. I was very upset about it for about four or five months afterwards because I thought that I had lost my manhood.[12]

Leo, having spent the bulk of his adolescent and adult years behind bars, devised a strategy to avoid physical and sexual violence in prison.

> First of all you learn to form alliances. Secondly, there's a lot of manipulation too. Thirdly I suppose, and maybe it should have been first, is the fact that by being considered dangerous and being dangerous [to other inmates and staff, you avoid trouble]. [This is similar to the situation like] if a woman is known to know martial arts and use it and has a weapon, you gotta think twice about [attacking her]. But again, if she has the potential to do serious bodily damage to somebody, she'd be a lot better off than if she didn't. And again here, even though you don't, you do crazy things in prison. I found out, even not intentionally. When I took the guard hostage, you know, other inmates would think

well if he would do that to him [what would he do to me?] . . . So you walled up this mystique, a reputation that may not be all that true and just balance that enough with the fact that you will hurt somebody and you can back it [danger] off somehow. When I got to Marion [a prison with a reputation for housing very dangerous inmates], everybody had the same kind of bad ass reps. You didn't know what the other guy was about. You knew if you went to Marion there was a problem somewhere. Everyday you woke up there was sort of a tension there and there was always something going down between factions and stuff. It was so small you always had to be there. Even if it wasn't your beef you could get stabbed. You could get burnt in your cell and all these kind [of things], so every day it was there. And there was a lot of brutal killings there, even though there wasn't as many stabbings, there was a lot of brutal murders right in front of everybody. And the guards were more keyed up to the tension involved and they were more [tense] . . . so everything was different. Because everyday you woke up in Marion – I used to get up very early – like I knew these doors popped [open] at certain times. You didn't know what anybody else was thinking at that time in the morning so you don't be laying in bed. If you're going to have some problem, you want to have it when you're awake. Yeah, I was conscious [of fear]. I made sure I got up before the door [popped open]. I was ready to go to the mess hall. I avoided certain places at times when I knew there was definitely going to be a problem. Like I knew this one was going to be stabbed in the movie or something like that, I wouldn't go to the movies that night. If I heard that there was a lot of escape possibility, you could get tracers [bullets] shot at you and everything else in the yard, so if I knew these things [about impending danger] I would avoid those . . . So that was probably the worst experience I had as far as having to be totally

aware every day of my life, every minute. It was nice
when it [the prison] got locked up at night. Nine o'clock
and you were locked in. You don't have to be on guard
so much.

Danger lurks in prison; it haunts the corridors placing guards
and inmates alike on alert. And it is the place men know they
will be afraid, and for good reason. But the majority of men
never experience being locked up. Most men continue to find
the outside world a relatively safe place, until, perhaps, they
have are seriously threatened or severely injured. If men
had been badly hurt, particularly recently, they could talk
about being afraid and uneasy in public. Men spoke about
the shock of feeling vulnerable on the street, which they
generally found alien to their everyday lives. Geoff, a 6'
2" actor, remembered, while discussing an assault, being
menaced on a train one night when returning from his job
with a London theatre company. While he initially felt fearful
after the incident on the train, he eventually resumed using
the train without much thought to his safety.

It took me a while to get over that incident. But I
had completely forgotten about it. At the time I was
attacked, I was completely blasé about it, my safety.
I mean that's why I was taking the short cut home
past the school where there's a very dark street. I did
something which I never do. I called into [the pub]. I
was very thirsty and I called into the pub right outside
Finsbury Park tube which is on the way home, and I had
a very quick pint and left there. I mean it was just before
11.00 and nobody else was leaving. That's how I know
the time and I came out of there and I just turned the
corner to walk north. There were three chaps coming
towards me . . . I'm sure it was them. And I got the
feeling that I was somehow checked out. [He was
wearing a Walkman and stopped listening and hung
the earphones around his neck.] You know, the way

people come that bit too close to you. You just feel like you're being watched or whatever. And they were big, they're as tall as I am and sort of solid. Then of course, they kept going. I kept going. I just relaxed again and a couple of times I crossed streets taking these short cuts. I thought I heard footsteps behind me. I remember at one stage I looked around and I saw a chap running down the street behind me. He was obviously in a hurry. He could have been going to follow me then changed his mind or whatever. But it looked like he was just sort of disappearing quickly. That's when I made the fatal turn. I took another left turn which was along this quiet street. They waited until I had just reached the wall of the school. No houses, except on the other side of the street, but before that there were houses on both sides. As I said what amazed me most, I was just walking along and suddenly they were there. I mean I didn't hear anything behind. I heard a quick sort [of noise, whoosh]. And one chap appeared in front of me and said give us your money or whatever. I sort of backed away from him and I turned around just in time to see the other two coming. I don't know how long it went on, it might have been a half a minute or whatever. There was a lot of kicking and punching and I remembered that I had my pay packet on me. I really let fly as much as I could. There seemed to be blows coming from every direction. Then the three of them just looked at each other and suddenly took off. I was in such a state of shock I didn't realise for virtually 7 or 8 minutes afterwards that they'd actually taken the bag. I mean I was just going around in a daze.

Geoff increased his surveillance for danger after the attack. This precaution extended to his home.

Every night when I come in [from work] I'm always wary. Whether or not there's the chance of anybody

> being in the flat, kind of waiting for me. I'll always leave a light on which my flatmate wants me to do anyway, because she's been burgled. [Now] I put my head in the door [laughs] to check the front room and the bedroom and then I sort of walk down towards the back room, the lounge and the kitchen. I mean I'm not totally paranoid about . . . I'm not shaking. I'm not in great fear or anything but I'm just cautious in case. I just sort of barged in [before the attack], threw things and didn't think about it.

Men I interviewed who had been physically assaulted, especially those with serious injuries, suddenly found they could not take their safety for granted. This realisation comes as a surprise and causes a marked change in their behaviour immediately after the assault. Those gravely injured remain concerned on some level as part of their everyday avoidance of danger. Clive and Tony described their attacks in Chapter 4 (pp. 74-8). Both seriously stabbed, they experienced acute anxiety immediately afterwards. They became irritable, had difficulty sleeping and lived with recurring physical problems relating to their injuries. So did Frank, who was attacked in a disco by a man who smashed a pint beer glass into his face.

These men experience the assault and subsequent feelings of vulnerability as an affront to their masculinity. Men are expected to be able to put up a good fight, like Geoff, and fend off their attackers. Tony, because he 'lost' the fight, did not know how to tell his son about the attack.

> I didn't feel bad about telling him. I just didn't want to tell him. I felt that I was sort of macho to him, you know, a tough guy. I just felt that I wasn't the sort of tough guy that I make out [to be]. I just felt that. I felt that [that he was a tough guy] about my dad. My dad this, my dad that. Now I feel I'm not the toughie I used to be to him.

MEN, MASCULINITY AND SAFETY

Clive, whose visible scars are quite horrific, has to deal with some friends and strangers telling him how they would have handled the fight, and won. 'They start telling you what they would do.' As adults, most men are beholden to the image that the 'real man' always overpowers his opponent.

Alan, an 18-year-old North London resident, became aware of dangers for women after his sister was raped, but did not feel that he was at risk to sexual assault.

> No, after what happened to my sister I didn't feel more vulnerable. I felt that I was responsible for making sure that either of my sisters or my friends got home at night safely. Even if they only lived around the corner I insisted on driving them home. I never actually thought of anything happening to me.

After an incident where he was robbed and physically threatened with a knife and hammer by two young men, he did feel at risk.

> I do go out at night but only if I can use the car or if I'm not on my own. I don't like going into pubs and things where there are a lot of people.

Feelings of vulnerability arise because of direct experience with violence, or may arise when a man feels vulnerable because of who he is. Some men feel threatened because they realise they are targets for others' hatred because they are gay, unemployed, physically disabled or a member of a religious or racial group. The next chapter explores how racial, sexual and homophobic violence affects the lives of men as well as women.

Chapter seven
CLIMATES OF UNSAFETY

Criminological debates rage about the reasons that comparatively high proportions of people of colour are arrested and imprisoned. Public discussions about crime and race, therefore, become focused almost exclusively on alleged perpetrators of violence.[1] People of colour who are subjected to personal violence rarely figure in academic meditations. The discipline of criminology is also strangely silent about violence against gay men and lesbians. An unspoken message is that this will remain a private burden of those who are not heterosexual. And it was radical feminists, not criminologists, who put violence against women on to the public agenda. That silence was shattered revealing the pervasive, yet hidden, context of sexual violence within which all women live.

I have already argued that women as women have a special relationship to danger. Women's precautions, taken in both public and private places, are acknowledgements of their relationship to threat and danger. In many ways, women's concern for their physical and sexual safety is such a part of their everyday lives as to render caution just good common sense.

Crime prevention literature acknowledges the special status of women as targets of violence. The recognition of women's vulnerability to sexual violence underlines protection advice. Despite the overwhelming evidence of danger at the hands of non-strangers, messages about self-protection and safety focus on the threat of stranger violence. The advice given suggests that violence, though random, can be avoided. Implicitly, those who do not avoid violence are therefore blamed for their encounters with danger.

This chapter illustrates the special awareness people of colour and gay men and lesbians have of their fragile relationship to safety. Negotiating the threat and experience of violence, I argue, becomes an arena for individual and collective struggles against private and collective dominance that is based largely within structures of advantage derived from race and heterosexuality. I do not suppose that each of us is simply experiencing the world as a 'female', or as an Afro-Caribbean, or as a lesbian. We are simultaneously female, black and lesbian; male, white and heterosexual, and so forth. It is how the following women and men recognise their vulnerability to danger and the silencing of that recognition through the public discourse about danger and criminality that is of interest here.

TARGETS OF VIOLENCE

Few white people think of themselves as having 'white' experience. To articulate racial awareness, in many ways, is to articulate what it means to be of a minority, 'of colour' in a context that supposedly knows no colour. To the white majority, people of colour pose a potential risk to safety. Avoiding contact with people of colour keeps the dangerous strangers at bay. The public façade of racial awareness associates 'whiteness' with safety, at least for the majority population.

In public, we scan for visual signs of possible trouble. The more varied and diverse an area, the more sophisticated some residents become in sorting risk, especially if threats are supposed to come from strangers. Take for example how we use race as a way of reading and managing potential danger. Susan Smith, in a study of Birmingham, England, shows how race and ethnicity are used by residents in a multi-racial community as a practical means of reducing perceived risks of violence.[2] Within environments where there are many people and many opportunities to fear the unknown, 'crude distinctions between white, black and brown' were the commonest ways for residents to spot who is potentially safe.

Sally Merry, in her study of an ethnically diverse housing project in Philadelphia, describes how residents monitor danger through the filters of their racial and ethnic social networks.[3] Crime, she suggests, 'serves as an idiom for expressing and legitimating the fear of the strange and the unknown.'[4] Residents, mostly white, Chinese and black, generally avoided members of other racial groups because their social networks, including the gossip about crime, extended into their wider ethnic communities. Those who felt most safe, young black men, used their reputations for violent retaliation as one form of protection, as well as their extensive street networks to provide information about 'who' everyone was, where they were likely to live, and their kinship and friendship patterns in case something did happen. By excluding those who are considered unsafe along racial lines, as the majority of residents seemed to do, then the stereotypes of danger magnified the social distances among many different peoples.

Fear and separation may take uglier forms in the use of active racial taunts, harassments and assaults. Assailants are as likely to be neighbours, employers, customers, schoolmates, fellow workers, or trainees as they are strangers. In spotting the dangers of the skin, so to speak, the practical reality of pursuing safety is achieved through avenues that take their mental maps from racialism. Steve, in recalling one incident as a child, describes how he was told, as a white person, that black might be dangerous.

> It was in Florida with my father. The family went down to visit his parents. We were driving by and we passed some sort of Dairy Queen [ice-cream fast food] or something. There were these blacks who

were outside eating ice-cream. My father said, 'Lock the doors.' And I said, 'Why?' And he said, 'Well, it's not safe.' I was like, 'They're just people.' 'Yes, but we want to keep ourselves safe.' I said like, 'What about Martin Luther King and Booker T. Washington?' and I let out my whole list of all the names of the great black people – most of them men – that I had been inculcated with in my liberal elementary school. And he said, 'Yes, well, that's different. These people are a threat to us.'

When threat becomes reality – an assailant, black; the attacked, white – one particularly powerful stereotype of danger comes to life. Tony, stabbed in a failed robbery attempt by two young black men, spoke bitterly about his increased racism, where he now treats all black men as potentially dangerous. His initial reaction to his assailants was that they were 'just kids, sort of my children's ages.' Afterwards when he was slow to recover from wounds that became infected, he turned his anger and resentment to all black men. John also had difficulty dealing with black men after his assault.

> There's a little peephole and [someone] knocked on the door. Every time I hear a noise my heart misses a beat. [I]went to the door and looked out the peephole and it was a black chap. So of course that then sent me back . . . When I went to the living room I was sort of shaking, like for a half an hour or so.

One white, middle-aged professional writer, also attacked by two young black men, was surprised by his racist reactions. While he was recovering from a serious head injury, he spoke to some close black friends about his wariness of Afro-Caribbean men. He was able to understand his responses in the context of racial hatred and the readily available account of crime as associated with the actions of young black men.

Residual fear of one's attackers, especially of those who visually resemble their attackers, is a common reaction of those victimised by serious violence. Women, for instance, often carry a fear of all men at least for some period of time following a sexual assault. Yet the fear and hatred of one's attackers can all too easily fit into the public discourse about crime. Those attacked by young black men may publicly express their outrage. But if the attack does not fit into the stereotype, then the victim bears the resentment and pain silently.

Frank, an Afro-Caribbean 23-year-old North Londoner, was punched in the face by a white man at a night club on his 21st birthday.

> The guy was white. I was frightened of that [running into him]. I'm still affected now. It's got better but at first. I can't recognise this bloke, he can be anybody. I've got a rough idea of what he looks like from someone else telling me a rough description, but I don't know. So [when I meet] anyone who fits that description, I'm half thinking, 'Is he going to jump out on me?'

Frank only had a rough idea what his assailant looked like, and the most distinctive feature was that he was white. Frank felt additional vulnerability because he perceived that the decision not to charge the suspect was a reflection of police racism. His own experience with the police taught him that some people are detained for questioning, even when they are innocent.

> D'ya know what I mean? I was bitter about that. I wasn't really pleased because I felt that they [the police] held him for three hours. This guy had a record for having done it before, and he was actually on a charge again . . . In the meantime he'd done this to me . . . And they held him for three hours . . . I remember getting arrested once. It was a big fight and someone said I was there. They [the police] come and held me for thirty hours. I'd been at a nightclub the

> night before . . . They had no reason to hold me, yet they did. And this guy who's done this serious assault, and who's done it a couple of times before and they held him for three hours and they let him go. None of this sweating him out . . . Racist? I dunno?

His assailant remains anonymous, and the uncomfortable questions about the possible racial motivations for the attack remain unanswered.

Ricardo, who earlier spoke about the beatings he experienced whilst growing up because he was Puerto Rican, learnt martial arts.

> To protect myself against anybody, mostly white people [men?]. I had a lot of trouble with whites because I was Puerto Rican.

Frank and Ricardo are conscious about the possiblity of being a target of someone's racial hatred; John did not feel he was a target of assault because he was white, but because he was perceived as gay.

> We're not really sure why it's all happened. When they [the assailants] came in and started bashing me up, they'd obviously been watching us. Two blokes living in a flat, presumed we were gay . . . I don't know. The things they were saying were like, 'You two are queer. Get out we don't want you around in this neighbourhood,' and that sort of thing.

Fred, who worked in a gay bar in Massachusetts, experienced violence from customers and from men who purposely went to the bar to 'cause trouble' for gay men.

> When I used to work down at the bar, I was the one responsible for calling the police, and the police never came. If they did come, it was [too] late. A lot of time they'd give us a hassle; so we just wanted to handle

things ourselves. Which usually meant people getting hurt, either my staff getting hurt, or me getting hurt.

Authorities such as the police and government or school officials, reinforce the right of individuals to threaten others if they themselves act in a similar fashion or fail to intervene in a positive way on behalf of the aggrieved. If no one in authority will remedy violent behaviour, one must shore up his or her internal resources and take additional precaution. Even when official responses to complaints of violence do lead to criminal charges, and individual situations are remedied, the climate of racial or anti-homosexual hatred within which the violence occurred still exists unfettered.

To some, the authorities themselves constitute a threat from which they need protection. Robert recalls a particularly frightening encounter with a police officer.

> Well, I was arrested by a trooper for driving fast. Got put in the trunk of his car with handcuffs and that time I didn't know where that trunk was going to open up. To me that's one of the worst things that ever happened. [With respect to people in authority] you have to respect them but there's a fear that goes with it and that's a fear that they're just as crazy as any other human being. They can go nuts just as much as anybody else.

Similar to women's awareness of sexual unsafety, people of colour and gay men and lesbians acknowledge their special vulnerability to attack. Fred's experiences of being assaulted suggest a pattern of harassment women commonly experience:

> I was assaulted on Main Street about five years ago. Someone came up behind me and started screaming, 'Faggot,' and punched me on the side of the head. I fell unconscious on to Main Street. There was a police

officer around the other corner and he walked away. That was pretty scary, because I didn't know what was going on. I tried reporting it to the police and they gave me a really hard time. That was scary because it was just, like random. There have been other times when I've been real scared. A couple of months ago, I was on Main Street on the telephone calling for a ride and a car-load of guys came over and started screaming they were going to kill me, and they knew what to do with faggots, and so on. Luckily, they eventually went away. Another time I was coming home from the bar and there was a van-load of men – they usually come in packs – and they were throwing beer bottles at me as I was walking in front of Beech Street. It was really late. It was like 1 o'clock at night and I had nowhere to go, and I certainly wasn't going to outrun this van. I was lucky their aim was bad.

If someone sees themselves as less powerful, it makes sense to attribute victimisation to the prejudice of those in power. Robert speaks about his awareness of being Hispanic:

I was talking about this to my sister . . . It was sort of like being Puerto Rican and I speak English well enough to communicate and have people not even know I'm Puerto Rican necessarily. Finding out that you're Puerto Rican does a number on people who have something against Puerto Ricans. It has nothing to do with my speaking any broken English, so that's when I know that it's something racial, you know. There's something – you don't know why somebody has this against you and it's not over communication or even status in a sense. But there have been things [incidents of differential treatment], probably more here in [Massachusetts] than in New York City. In New York City I could be a poor slob but I still get to be more than a poor slob. I can do things without having people say, 'Oh, he's Puerto

Rican, maybe we won't give him a shot.' That kind of thing. I was unemployed for two years and looking for work and having some experience dabbling into a lot of different things, but never really had a shot at any one of them. So I just feel like that's sort of my lot in life until I got into what I'm doing [now]. And that was through a friend . . . There's a lot of prejudging, that's prejudice, that's just people that assume, you know, so and so's one of *these*.

Evidence of the silence of all women, people of colour and gay men to complain about criminal violence to the police amply supports the suspicion of the powerless about the quality and accessibility of public protection. Frank comments about his attack by a white man:

You know, divide and rule, that's the way I see it. You know, keep them divided, keep them battling against each other, keep them in ignorance and we'll maintain power. I can almost see it happening around me all the time.

Pam adds:

Violence can be rape, or a sexually-assaultive remark of one kind or another. Women are expected to accept that. As a lesbian, I put up with homophobia, that's institutionalised. So is sexism. The pervasiveness is alarming. One of the most important parts about safety is that I'm not sure if it's possible for women to know what safety is, because women experience violence all their lives. You can be safer, but . . .

During childhood and young adulthood, many of us understand that we occupy a power in a hierarchically arranged society. Jockeying for power may involve the use of force. But more often, we identify ways in which to avoid potential violence because we are conscious of being at risk merely because we are 'legitimate' targets. And to a large extent, our expertise in precaution attests to our survival skills.

SURVIVING CLIMATES OF DANGER

Liz Kelly, in her eloquent treatise on sexual violence,[5] suggests that women use a variety of coping and resistance strategies to manage such experiences. Women live with sexual danger as the frame of their public and private lives. While these survival strategies are similar to those all of use in one form or another, their use underscores the active resistance to violence. The process of resistance is one that spans a lifetime.

Kelly suggests that women's coping strategies are active, positive challenges to men's private power. Most often at the hands of known others, experiences of unsafety elude the 'official' definitions of sexual violence held by the law or helping agencies. Kelly lists a number of techniques women use to manage sexual violence and danger. Survival strategies represent a process of progressive awareness about confronting the daily damage caused by the existence of rampant sexual violence.

Resistance becomes politicised when individually experienced indignities come to be understood as collective degradation. As people identify the processes in surviving violence, they can begin to understand the context within which their abuse is encouraged.

Similar to women's relationship to male society, the process of coping and resisting exists for people of colour within a white society and for lesbians and gay men within a heterosexual society. Fred describes how he manages to forget about constant harassment because he is gay – a strategy Kelly suggests minimises the damage of constant abuse.

> Things happen to me and I'll tell friends of mine who are straight about it and they'll be horrified. And they'll

remember three weeks later, while I will have forgotten it in the next week. I had an experience where someone called me and said, 'What happened? Are you all right?' And I was like, 'Oh, my God, did something happen to me that I don't know about? What? ' It turned out it was an incident with those guys in a truck [where they were telling me they were going to kill me]. I mean, how many incidents have there been? Most straight people don't have people driving up to them screaming, 'We're gonna kill you [because you are gay].'

Women typically experience – too many times even to note – men screaming at them saying they want to 'fuck' them. Racial harassment, a daily experience for some, also takes its toll. 'There are youngsters shouting "black bastard", or "Paki go home" and one is only 4 years old,' stated one Asian man living in Leicester, England. His wife added: 'They break the windows, break the fence, put fireworks through the letterbox, empty the bin in the back yard.' This couple, fearing the everyday violence on their housing estate, have recently had an 'emergency panic button' installed so that they may summon the police when trouble starts. While the racist graffiti is removed within 24 hours as part of Leicester council's campaign against racial attacks, the couple remain behind closed doors in fear. The climate of racial hatred solidifies fear. Pushing the panic button, calls the police *after* violence begins.

Some resistance strategies involve blocking out the effects of the abuse. Kim, a West Indian woman living in Hackney, England, commented that, 'If there would be those [racist] comments, I don't hear them.' Rachel, a white lesbian living in Massachusetts, spoke of harassment she received because of her sexuality.

> I think that most of the cases that come to mind are drunken males, red-neck men, good ol' boys, just saying things [like] 'fucking lesbians', and stuff like that. It was

never a physical threat. Just something that they had to say to make themselves feel manly, I guess.

Searching for a way to justify abusive treatment, Rachel blames masculinity and drink for the violence she receives, not the wider expectations of heterosexuality. Pam, a white lesbian also living in Massachusetts, draws a distinction between the kinds of harassment she receives:

> If they're [the comments] just misogynistic, I feel one way. If they are homophobic, I feel worse, more threatened.

Just as women are used to receiving harassment on the street or in the form of an obscene phone call, so too do some experiences of gays or minorities become categorised as part of the common annoyances and minor threats linked with being an 'other'. The two men, one gay, one Asian, who reported receiving threatening phone calls directed at their sexuality or their race respectively, attribute these calls to 'psychopaths' or 'nutters'. Fred reports:

> I've gotten harassing phone calls. I've had people calling my house and screaming, 'Fag!' into the phone and stuff, but I'm not really sure what that's from. I think it's just that I lucked out and got a psychopath or it's someone who saw my name in a newspaper or something.

While in general women use more elaborate precautionary strategies for self-protection than men, some lesbians and gay men develop precautionary strategies to protect themselves specifically from homophobic violence. Still others may not disclose their homosexuality for fear of social and physical retaliation. Fred speaks about how he changed his appearance.

> For one thing, I started dressing safer: a lot of khakis and button-downs and loafers. I'm really thin and I think that has a lot to do with it, 'cause there's a cultural perception that all fags are really skinny. Somatically, as a physical type, I must look very gay, and I'm certainly not a threatening kind of person . . . So I dress safer.

Rachel comments about how others take her appearance:

> I am mistaken for a male a lot . . . As a matter of fact, it always surprises me when people mistake me for a female . . . like I'm a woman right away surprises me because it's something new. Generally the harassment that comes around mistaking me for a male is people call me a fag which is a kind of funny thing or they'll say things like, 'Let your hair grow,' or, 'Why don't you dress different if you're a woman.' . . . I feel the least safe walking in and out of gay bars. It worries me that people are watching the door, straight people [men?] out to ambush [me] or something like that.

Coping strategies combine techniques to minimise being spotted as a potential target together with strategies to distance oneself from situations where one may confront danger.

It is at the crossroads of being a target and experiencing violence that the process of individualising safety begins. Silence about the danger of being gay and lesbian or being a person of colour is the result. The management of the indignity and the danger of being a target for violence is largely carried by people as an unspoken expectation of ordinary life. It is only when stepping outside of the target status that people can experience the freedom associated with not being on guard. Women who, for instance, are mistaken for men find distinct advantages among the annoyances and difficulties of being treated as males. Using the illusion of a male body, women find that they are largely able to avoid the constraints and confinement of being a woman. By passing as men, these women feel they can escape the threat of physical and sexual violence they would expect to experience from men.[6]

Gordon, a 23-year-old gay man living in Massachusetts, sees physical strength and a 'man-like' appearance as mitigating violence against him.

> Visually I am a more dominating figure . . . I'm damn lucky I'm big. And going to the gym and working out is one of the things that helps to accentuate my size. Having the height advantage, it's a big advantage. And I do. That's one of the reasons I work out, is to perpetuate, no, to keep that [bodily image] going . . . I like to think that I don't come up in the stereotypic ways of gay men, so when I walk down the street I don't see myself as attracting attention in that sense, therefore limiting my vulnerability that way . . . The man who walks with a wiggle or talks with a lisp – and I know of a number of men like that – I think they have a whole hell of a lot more to worry about than I do.

Pam, a lesbian living in Massachusetts, draws a connection between being a woman and a lesbian.

> As a woman, I'm always on the look-out for . . . I don't know what being safe means. I feel safer there [in this North shore town] than other places I've lived. Specifically as a lesbian . . . it's a double wammy: woman and lesbian. I'm pretty identifiable as a lesbian except for those hets with blinders on who never [see anything] and I don't generally display affection on the street because we live there. That's not being safe.

So while some lesbian women may escape many of the traps of heterosexuality – dressing 'appropriately' female – the dangers of defying male control over their sexuality bring other dangers. Micki suggests that attempting to eliminate sexualised encounters with men brings some, albeit limited, safety.

> I guess I feel safer not because I'm a lesbian . . . I guess, maybe, because I'm beginning to realise that I don't have to play the games with men. And I can just say 'go away'. In that way, I don't have to feel badly about defending myself if I have to. I don't feel I have to be nice to men. But in terms of risk, I don't think I'm any less at risk than anybody else – or probably a little more, because of anti-gay and lesbian physical abuse. It [the abuse] could be stone throwing, it could be sexual assault too.

Anticipation of violence, manifest in the conscious or unconscious use of precaution, reflects the power and influence of racism, sexism and homophobia today. Certainly, I do not assume that those who are male, white and heterosexual never confront violence. They do. The time, effort and anxiety of having to *think* about safety, day-in and day-out, is different. Naming danger is the first step in demanding a right to be autonomous and asserting the power to name experiences of unsafety as extensions of social degradation. In the final chapter, we shall take a look at the concept of protection in the light of the kinds of danger many of us face today, and attempt to articulate what preventing 'crime' really means.

Chapter eight
SAFETY AND PROTECTION IN MODERN SOCIETY

Woven through these chapters have been themes which raise some broad issues about protection and safety which need public attention as well as debate by our policy makers in crime prevention. I would like to open up these issues in this final chapter.

We gather our knowledge of danger and of violence in private, yet it is in the public domain that the thinking about crime and violence takes place. The public debate about crime, in too many respects, wrongly silences our private understandings about personal danger. And the way in which anxiety about safety is publicly expressed serves to separate the fear of crime from our private knowledge about danger. For despite the clear evidence that the risk of interpersonal violence is overwhelmingly from those near and dear to us, we all seem to worry more about threats from strangers.

Of course, safety in public places is a real and important concern for us. Those who speak in this book report many examples of public violence: purses snatched, personal robberies, stabbings, sexual assaults. This is the fodder of headline news, and there is, as Geoffrey Pearson has shown, a long history of attention devoted to the perceived danger of public space.[1] And yet, when asked about experiences and feelings of danger, these people also speak about unsafe situations, which involve relatives, lovers, friends, co-workers, or acquaintances. They also involve the danger associated with being female, homosexual or of colour. Threats and violence experienced in these situations are more likely to be silently endured. Rarely are the police informed about private danger and threat.

But when we speak about fear of crime, why do we exclude the anxiety and fear caused by experiences of private danger? To talk about fear of crime, instead of fear of danger, means that criminologists can only discuss the hazards of the 'public'. Criminologists and the popular press now recognise the fear of crime as a social problem in its own right, quite separate from actual experience.[2] Its impact on people's lives through, for example, the tactics of precaution or the purchase of security devices is well documented.[3] Fear and anxiety about crime is treated by many criminologists and others as a malady of modern society, a disease to be cured. While researchers debate whether fear is linked to actual risk of danger, the underlying assumption is that anxiety about danger is somehow alien to the lives of citizens in so-called civilised societies.

Criminologists reassure us that we overestimate the likelihood of encountering criminal violence ourselves because violent offences comprise only a small proportion of those crimes reported to the police. Genuine fear of crime, that which stems from the aftermath of criminal victimisation, may be reduced, according to popular thinking, by offering support and assistance to victims.[4] We must look elsewhere, researchers suggest, to explore the factors that contribute to citizen anxiety about crime.

One widely held view is that community disorder increases people's fears about crime.[5] In areas with high levels of graffiti, public drunkenness, or litter, for instance, people are more concerned about their safety in public.[6] Another theory, the 'community concern' perspective, posits that fear of crime is locally based in an awareness of the overall problems within a community, such as poor sanitation or education.[7] According to this perspective, fear of crime will decrease alongside the ability of members of a community to work together to change their environment for the better. A third perspective supports the connection between fear of crime and knowledge about how the effects of crime are perceived by specific groups. Learning about crime, through gossip or newsprint, is more likely to worry those who are already vulnerable, such as women and the elderly.[8] All three perspectives treat fear of crime as a *perceived* vulnerability, unconnected to actual experience. To date, only the local crime surveys conducted in inner London by Jock Young and his associates provide evidence which suggests that fear is directly related to experiences of crime.[9]

So what measures are seen to provide the antidotes to what is perceived to be fear of crime? In many respects, the police have become the front-runners in tackling that fear. Ideas put forth by James Wilson and George Kelling in 1982 propose that fear is related to disorder, and the police, as the internal arm of the state responsible for order, can take the lead in restoring feelings of security. Experiments in 'fear reduction', such as those conducted by the Police Foundation in Newark, New Jersey and Houston, Texas, were spearheaded by police initiatives, yet the results of these experiments suggest that levels of fear were not significantly reduced by this approach.[10]

For the police, allaying citizen fear about crime has become a barometer of success. If the police can appear to be more sensitive and accessible to the public, they may be better able to reduce anxiety about crime because people will feel that they can rely on the police for protection. The debate is heated about how successful police efforts are likely to be and crucial to that debate is just how confident people are in the ability of the police to stop crime. Indifferent or harsh treatment of minorities and women by the police has eroded trust in their ability to provide impartial assistance. And even the best intentioned police supervisors can never guarantee the sensitivity of each officer working the street.

The police are also criticised for not faring very well in the overall fight in the war on crime. Feminists have criticised with some force, the ways in which police approached their treatment of sexually or physically assaulted women. The police have not been deaf to critics. Nowadays, they are eager to show how sympathetic they are to the problems of women, in particular, in the areas of sexual assault and domestic violence. As a result, many police forces have redesigned the training of recruits, some require officers to submit written reports of family disputes, and many have changed their procedures of hearing complaints of sexual assault, agreeing on a number of occasions to undergo the scrutiny of academic researchers. These changed procedures, though, do not actually protect women from sexual or physical attack prior to police intervention. The police have also been criticised for ignoring racially motivated attacks. In some jurisdictions as well, they have tried to tackle complaints about racial harassment that have rarely been considered appropriate situations for police intervention.

In many respects, the police, in becoming more responsive to the types of crimes assumed to fuel the most fear, have widened their crime prevention role in the community and to some extent the expectations of the public for protection. They visit schools and instruct children about staying away from strangers. In many forces, local crime prevention officers will inspect homes, suggesting improvements to deter burglars. The police have also broadened their crime prevention advice about adequate security hardware and may suggest some simple rules for safety. These enlightened changes in policing strategies and attitudes will hopefully help to reassure citizens about their own safety both in public places and within their homes.

Yet, so little of what people define as crime comes to the attention of the police, and still fewer situations experienced as dangerous or threatening come to any public attention at all. As they have illustrated throughout the previous chapters, people's ways of understanding danger is complex, and highly private, grounded in a lifetime of experience. Nevertheless, whenever the problems of crime and violence are publicly addressed, the discussion turns to the adequacy of the police and policing as the starting point in the dialogue, thus conflating *public* safety with private danger. Crime, stereotypically, strikes at random. Strangers await the opportunity to catch unsuspecting victims off-guard and the police – at least when criminal victimisation is involved – provide protection as the thin blue line between victim and offender.

Our precautionary strategies, though, become private ingredients in a search for safety that we know the police cannot provide. We often feel that the police should not be involved in many threatening and dangerous events, because these are considered private matters, however frightening and abusive they may be. Or we may think that even if we do request outside intervention, we will be subjected to subsequent embarrassment, humiliation and exposure as *victims*.

This private face of danger – that which arises from those most familiar – becomes obscured by the focus on public safety. Indeed, there is a serious mismatch between public discourse on crime and private knowledge about danger. The most obvious example of this mismatch lies within women's experiences and it cannot be bridged by expanding women's repertoire of precautions: shrill alarms, self-defence courses, advance planning, better lighting. Such solutions mask and foster the most significant threat to women's safety: those men with whom women are familial and familiar. For women, the private danger and violence from those men are so common that they challenge the very dialogue about crime. Rather than lack of police protection, it is the very structure of women's lives that continually places them at risk of danger.

Even when the police are involved in dangerous situations, such as domestic violence or racial harassment, they cannot provide us with remedies to counteract the actual causes of violence. For it is, finally, the very vulnerability of women to attack by partners, or that of people of colour to attack by whites, that is essential to maintain society's imbalance of personal power. But by calling for increased police intervention, we are handing greater power to the police, who are often themselves immune from scrutiny, to resolve instances of violence that stem from the very core of everyday social relations.

How can we make sense of such a claim as this? One way is the analysis of gender and safety I have adopted in this book. Such an analysis provides a framework for describing the emotional, social and financial costs of negotiating subordination in everyday life: what it means to experience being a target of violence. The burden of safety, we learn, falls on the shoulders of individual women, both in their private and public lives; precautions are integral to women's safe passage through daily existence, and women quietly accept the inconveniences that accompany precautions. By using this framework to explore how people of colour, straight and gay men, and lesbians cope with the threat and experience of danger, I hope to open up the discussions about how people understand their relationship to systems of dominance founded within structures of race, gender and heterosexuality.

Danger, I feel, is at the heart of most people's everyday lives. As a feminist, I have been interested in making public women's private experiences of men's violence. As a criminologist, I now wish to make explicit the missed connection between public crime and private danger. We tenaciously cling to the myth that only a stranger would harm us. Regardless of the best intentions of the police, most of their efforts to protect us from danger are 'band-aid' solutions, offering some comfort, but seldom protection, to those who might ask for assistance.

Those involved in crime prevention do not set out to learn about danger from people's knowledge, rather they set out to lock out stranger crime. We are advised about how to reduce our vulnerability to crime by limiting our contact with those who choose to commit crime when in public or told to fortify the hardware in our homes. The home security industry, for example, is finding increased profits in this strategy. Between

1985 and 1989 in the UK, the retail sales of home security products nearly trebled in value.[11]

The security industry exploits the spotlight on fear of crime, offering a full range of devices promising to make us safer. Take a look in the local paper, magazine or Yellow Pages to see how home security is advertised. In my local Yellow Pages, for instance, I can refer to the sections entitled 'burglar alarms and security systems' or 'security services and equipment'. One company features a comforting pair of hands embracing a single family brick house. Another shows a man, dressed entirely in black, sneaking through a window. Clearly we are to assume he is a burglar. Yet another pictures a room in disarray, with the television smashed in, curtains ripped from the wall. Strangers must have entered.[12]

Crime prevention publicity and security hardware deny the overwhelming impact of experiences of private danger. So too has criminology which, as a discipline, has been slow to adapt its theories to incorporate the vast proportion of people's experiences of private danger into their discussions about crime.

What might crime prevention strategies based in an awareness of the nature of private danger look like? The best crime prevention must include mechanisms to teach people to confront abuses of power. We must all be agents for our own safety. Is it possible to teach children to protect themselves against the power of adults – uncles and fathers as well as strangers – to hurt them, while at the same time encouraging them to form bonds and relationships? I do not know. But we must be willing to find a way to explore the possibility of encouraging children, women and men, gay and straight, of all colours to resist unfettered, individual power.

One essential step is to acknowledge publicly the widespread existence of private violence. Despite police intervention at times of individual instances of danger and violence, collective vulnerability of those in less powerful positions, the real problem, remains unchanged. Criminologists and policy makers must wrestle with the thorny problems inequality encourages, not only in the public sector but in the private as well. The inequalities societies spawn and foster cannot as easily be swept away as litter and broken glass can. No matter how sensitive and sympathetic the police become, they will never be able to provide protection against everyday danger.

In the short term there are a few things we can do. First of all, we need to establish a new definition of the risk of danger. Rather than associate violence with our times in public places, we should think of risk as related to how often we find ourselves in the presence of others who have more power.

Such re-thinking of danger, violence and safety involves an exploration of personal and collective power and its abuses. We need to ask why, in such large numbers, women fear men. Why are people of colour so acutely aware of their vulnerability to attack because they are not white? Why do lesbians and gay men fear homophobic violence because of their choice of sexual partners? Obviously not all those who are in positions of greater relative power abuse that power, but far too many do. We need only to read back the tales told here of elaborate strategies so many people take for us to get a glimpse of how widespread and pervasive violence and danger are in their lives. The concerns of women, people of colour, lesbians and gay men do cross class boundaries, for those with greater incomes are by no means immune from danger from their friends, colleagues and intimates. Nor are they protected from being considered an appropriate target of hatred by strangers who wish specifically to abuse a woman, attack a person of colour, or hurt someone who chooses someone of their own gender as a sexual partner.

Ultimately, we must also ask why it is that those in positions of power use violence to keep those most vulnerable under control. Keeping people in fear is the weapon of authorities who have little to justify their greater position and prestige. We have no difficulty identifying the horror of the evil dictator who subjugates the ordinary citizen by the use of death squads, torture, or unlawful imprisonment. With recent changes in political climates in Eastern Europe bringing an embrace of Western-style capitalism, should there not be a sort of health warning: beware the underside of 'democracy' – the anxiety and fear of personal danger?

Breaking the silence about the danger of the private is one way of undermining the power of abusers. We must, therefore, rethink our strategies for punishing or sanctioning those who abuse their power. Turning to the criminal justice system to remedy all violations of personal safety is, I feel, unrealistic. The criminal justice system is geared to fact-finding around crime and criminal matters. We know that this system is unsuccessful in acting as the sole mediator of situations of violence, especially private violence.

Thus, we must examine how institutions, such as the criminal justice system, as resources of those holding greater collective power, in fact deny that it is many people, not just a select few, who abuse that power. We are horrified when fathers, uncles, brothers, friends, neighbours and colleagues are dangerous. But they are often labelled as psychologically unbalanced, different from the rest of us law-abiding citizens. Institutions, rather than offering protection against these kinds of violence, consistently deny the causal existence of sexual or racial danger and often tacitly accuse the recipient of such of courting violence. Institutional deafeners to complaints about danger are powerful silencers. So much so that, on an individual basis, managing danger is a fact of life.

Local initiatives have provided some respite from violence and we should learn from them. Battered women's refuges and shelters, for instance, no matter how sparsely furnished and under-financed, have offered many women safe passage from the danger of violent men. Of course, not all women who flee to refuges escape those violent men. Some return, hoping the men will change. Some return, knowing their emotional and financial ties are too strong to break, at least this time. Some return, only finally to leave for good.

Providing escape to some women, though, does not confront the structures that support women's economic, social and emotional dependence upon men. Promoting women's safety means promoting women's autonomy from men. It means challenging the silence around sexual violence, the ultimate weapon in women's social subordination.

Finally, and crucially, we must transfer our focus upon preventing crime, to concentrate upon preventing danger. Implicit in this approach is that action against structures of subordination, and specifically those which promote women's subordination, racism and homophobia, is positive action against criminal victimisation. This, perhaps, is the most difficult suggestion of all. But to refuse to re-think our beliefs about the balance of power between women and men, or about people of colour as somehow inferior or threatening, or about homosexuality as a threat to the family or family values, means that we will continue to place many in positions of danger.

The challenge of the 1990s will be to find mechanisms to alleviate the dangers accompanying unequal power. These mechanisms are not coming from the efforts of policy makers or from government initiatives on crime prevention. These mechanisms are coming from the experiences and creative thinking of people at the ground level. In many respects, we need to acknowledge the success of feminists who, despite all odds, meagre finances and initial community hostility, demanded that women be treated differently. It is possible to do much, much more.

NOTES

CHAPTER ONE

1 Data from crime surveys measure patterns of becoming a victim of crime, usually in the previous year. Victimisation surveys, as they are also called, indicate that most crime which people experience never comes to the attention of the police. Young men, according to these surveys, are found to be at the highest risk to personal violence than any other group. See M. Hindelang, M. Gottfredson, and J. Garofalo, *The Victims of Personal Crime*, Cambridge, MA, Ballinger Press, 1978.
2 Hindelang et al., op. cit., L. Cohen and M. Felson, 'Social change and crime rate trends: a routine activity approach', *American Sociological Review*, vol. 44, 1979, pp. 588–608.
3 E. A. Stanko, 'Fear of crime and the myth of the safe home: a feminist critique of criminology', in K. Yllo and M. Bograd, *Feminist Perspectives on Wife Abuse*, London, Sage, 1988.
4 The research is clear: women are more at risk from physical and sexual violence at the hands of men they know, than they are from strangers. See, for example, L. Kelly, *Surviving Sexual Violence*, Oxford, Polity Press, 1988; D. E. H. Russell, *Rape in Marriage*, New York, Macmillan, 1982; R. Warshaw, *I Never Called It Rape*, New York, Harper & Row, 1989; L. J. F Smith, *Concerns About Rape*, London, HMSO, 1989.
5 Kelly, op. cit.
6 The class was a seminar on safety and violence in everyday life. Not all of the student interviews are included in this book because of the varying competence of the student interviewees. Many of the interviews, though, provide a wealth of information supporting the arguments presented here.

7 My book, *Intimate Intrusions: Women's Experiences of Male Violence* (1985) examines how women's lives are permeated with experiences of male violence.

CHAPTER TWO

1 Research & Forecasts, Inc. with Ardy Friedberg, *America Afraid: How Fear of Crime Changes the Way We Live*, New York, New American Library, 1983, pp. 229–33; G. Hill, F. Howell and E. Driver, 'Gender, fear and protective handgun ownership', *Criminology*, vol. 23, no. 3, pp. 541–52, 1985.
2 P. Mayhew, N. A. Maung and C. Mirrlees-Black, *The 1992 British Crime Survey*, London, HMSO; US Department of Justice, *Report to the Nation on Crime and Justice*, 1988.

CHAPTER THREE

1 M. Hough and P. Mayhew, *The British Crime Survey*, London, HMSO, 1983; M. Hough and P. Mayhew, *Taking Account of Crime*, London, HMSO, 1985; for a thorough review of the literature, see P. Mayhew, 'The effects of crime: victims, the public and fear', in *Research on Victimisation*, Collected Studies in Criminological Research, Vol. XXIII, Strasbourg, Council of Europe, 1986, pp. 67–103.

CHAPTER FOUR

1 Dr. Liz Kelly, Child Sex Abuse Unit, North London Polytechnic, London, personal communication, 1990. See also, Kelly, op. cit., for an extensive review of the literature.
2 A. Burgess and L. Holmstrom, *Rape: Victims of Crisis*, Baltimore, MD, Bowie, 1974.
3 D. E. H. Russell, *The Politics of Rape*, New York, Free Press, 1973; A. Burgess and L. Holmstrom, 'Rape trauma syndrome', *American Journal of Orthopsychiat*, vol. 131, pp. 981–6, 1974.
4 US Department of Justice, *Report to the Nation on Crime and Justice*, Washington DC, US Government Printing Office, 1988, p. 29.
5 D. E. H. Russell, *Rape in Marriage*, New York, Macmillan, 1982.
6 Warshaw, op. cit.

NOTES

7 Hough and Mayhew (1983), op. cit.; Hough and Mayhew (1985), op. cit.; Mayhew, Dowds and Elliot, op. cit.; US Department of Justice, op. cit.

CHAPTER FIVE

1 See M. Gordon and S. Riger, *The Female Fear*, New York, Free Press, 1988.
2 See Kelly, op. cit.
3 Russell (1982), op. cit.
4 See J. Holland, C. Ramazanolu and S. Scott, 'Managing risk and experiencing danger: tensions between government AIDS educational policy and young women's sexuality', *Gender and Education*, July 1990.
5 Warshaw, op. cit.
6 Holland et al., op. cit.
7 C. M. Phillips, J. Stockdale and L. Joeman; *The Risks of Going to Work*, Suzy Lamplugh Trust, March 1989.
8 Cited in E. A. Stanko, *Intimate Intrusions: Women's Experience of Male Violence*, London, 1985, Unwin Hyman, pp. 61–2.
9 There are pilot schemes to discover ways to 'discourage' obscene phone callers. In one US area, phones now are equipped to provide the receiver with the number of the caller. By and large, similar to sexual harassment on the street, obscene phone calls are considered 'little annoyances' and are not taken seriously as another factor contributing to women's understanding of sexual vulnerability.
10 Gordon and Riger, op. cit.
11 S. Edwards, in J. Hanmer and M. Maynard, *Women, Violence and Social Control*, London, Macmillan, 1987, pp. 152–68.
12 E. Miller, *Street Woman*, Philadelphia, Temple University Press, 1986. The quote is from a personal communication.

CHAPTER SIX

1 Victimisation surveys consistently find that men report feeling safe on the street after dark. See, for example, Hindelang, Gottfredson and Garofalo (1978), op. cit.; M. Maxfield, *Fear of Crime in England and Wales*, London, HMSO, 1984; M. Gottfredson, *Victims of Crime: The Dimensions of Risk*, London, HMSO, 1984; W. Skogan and M. Maxfield, *Coping with Crime*, London, Sage, 1981; Hough and Mayhew (1983), op. cit.; Hough and Mayhew (1985), op. cit.; G. Chambers

and J. Tombs, *The British Crime Survey, Scotland*, Edinburgh, HMSO, 1984. For a thorough review of the research, see Mayhew, op. cit.
2 Maxfield, op. cit.
3 I conducted small-scale surveys in my classes at Clark University, Worcester, Massachusetts, for three years with consistent results. Using questionnaires, I asked what kind of crime concerned male and female students alike. The male students reported that they worried about possessions such as cars and stereos; the female students reported rape as their worry.
4 V. Seidler, 'Raging Bull', in *Achilles Heel*, no. 5, 1980, p.9.
5 T. Ryan, 'Roots of masculinity', in A. Metcalf and M. Humphries, *The Sexuality of Men*, London, Pluto, 1985, pp. 15–27.
6 G. A. Fine, *With the Boys*, Chicago, University of Chicago Press, 1987.
7 Finkelhor, op. cit.
8 A. N. Groth and T. Gary, 'Heterosexuality, homosexuality and pedophilia: sexual offences against children and adult sexual orientation', in A. M. Scacco (ed.), *Male Rape*, New York, AMS Press, 1982.
9 Gordon and Riger, op. cit.
10 Hough and Mayhew (1985), op. cit. These overall figures have not changed substantially in three subsequent crime surveys.
11 W. S. Wooden and J. Parker, *Men Behind Bars: Sexual Exploitation in Prison*, New York, Da Capo Press, 1982, p. 15.
12 D. Lockwood, *Prison Sexual Violence*, New York, Elsevier, 1980, p. 90–1.

CHAPTER SEVEN

1 See, for example, R. J. Herrnstein and J. Q. Wilson, *Crime and Human Nature*, New York, Simon & Schuster, 1985; E. Currie, *Confronting Crime*, New York, Pantheon, 1985; P. Gilroy, *There Ain't No Black in the Union Jack*, London, Hutchinson Educational: Unwin Hyman, 1987; J. Lea and J. Young, *What's to Be Done about Law and Order?*, London, Penguin, 1984.
2 S. J. Smith, 'Negotiating ethnicity in an uncertain environment', *Ethnic and Racial Studies*, vol. 7, no. 3, July 1984, pp. 360–73.
3 S. Merry, *Urban Danger: Life in a Neighbourhood of Strangers*, Philadelphia, Temple University Press, 1981.
4 Ibid., p. 14.
5 Kelly, op. cit.

NOTES

6   H. Devor, 'Gender blending females: women and sometimes men', in H. Brod and W. L. Williams (eds.) *New Gender Scholarship: Breaking Old Boundaries*, *American Behavioral Scientist*, vol. 31, no. 1, 1987.

CHAPTER EIGHT

1   Geoffrey Pearson, *Hooligan: A History of Respectable Fears*, London, Macmillan, 1983.
2   For a review of the literature, see J. Garofalo, 'Victimisation and the fear of crime', *Journal of Research in Crime and Delinquency*, vol. 16, 1979, pp. 80–97; Hindelang, Gottfredson and Garofalo, op. cit.; L. W. Kennedy and R. A. Silverman, 'Perceptions of social diversity and fear of crime', *Environment and Behaviour*, vol. 17, 1985, pp. 275–96; D. Lewis and G. Salem, *Fear of Crime: Incivility and the Production of a Social Problem*, Oxford, Transaction Books, 1986; Maxfield (1984), op. cit.; M. Maxfield, *Explaining Fear of Crime: Evidence from the 1984 British Crime Survey*, London, Home Office Research and Planning Unit Paper 43, 1988; S. Smith, *Crime, Space and Society*, Cambridge, Cambridge University Press, 1986. For an examination of the popularisation of the problem of fear, see M. Grade, *Report of the Working Group on the Fear of Crime*, London, Home Office Crime Prevention Unit, 1989.
3   P. Lavrakas and D. Lewis, 'Conceptualisation and measurement of citizens: crime prevention behaviours', *Journal of Research in Crime and Delinquency*, vol. 17, 1980, pp. 254–73; Gordon and Riger, op. cit.; Skogan and Maxfield, op. cit.
4   Trevor Bennett, 'Tackling fear of crime: a review of policy options', unpublished paper, May 1989.
5   See, for example, Skogan and Maxfield op. cit.; D. Lewis and M. Maxfield, 'Fear in the neighbourhoods: an investigation of the impact of crime', *Journal of Research in Crime and Delinquency*, vol. 17, 1980, pp. 160–89.
6   J. Wilson and G. Kelling, 'Broken windows', *The Atlantic Monthly*, vol. 249, 1982, p. 29.
7   J. Conklin, *The Impact of Crime*, New York, Macmillan, 1975; Lewis and Salem, op. cit.
8   Skogan and Maxfield, op. cit.; T. Tyler, 'Impact of directly and indirectly experienced events: the origin of crime-related judgements and behaviours', *Journal of Personality and Social Psychology*, vol. 39, no. 1, 1980, pp. 3–28.

9 T. Jones, B. MacLean and J. Young, *The Islington Crime Survey* London, Gower, 1986; *The Second Islington Crime Survey*, Middlesex Polytechnic, 1990.
10 T. Pate, W. Skogan and L. Sherman, *Fear of Crime and Policing*, Washington DC Police Foundation, 1985.
11 'Home Security', *Market Intelligence*, January 1990 report.
12 I am referring to the London East Yellow Pages, 1989.

BIBLIOGRAPHY

Bennett, T. (1989) 'Tackling fear of crime: a review of policy options', unpublished paper, University of Cambridge.

Burgess, A. and Holmstrom, L. (1974) *Rape: Victims of Crisis* (Baltimore, MD: Bowie).

Chambers, G. and Tombs, J. (1984) *The British Crime Survey: Scotland* (Edinburgh: HMSO).

Cohen, L. and Felson, M. (1979) 'Social change and crime rate trends: a routine activity approach', *American Sociological Review*, vol. 44, pp. 588–608.

Conklin, J. (1975) *The Impact of Crime* (New York: Macmillan).

Currie, E. (1985) *Confronting Crime* (New York: Pantheon).

Devor, H. (1987) 'Gender blending females: women and sometimes men', in H. Brod and W. Williams (eds) *New Gender Scholarship: Breaking Old Boundaries, American Behavioral Scientist*, vol. 31, no. 1.

Edwards, S. (1987) 'Provoking her own demise: from common assault to homicide', in J. Hanmer and M. Maynard (eds), *Women, Violence and Social Control* (London: Macmillan), pp. 152–168.

Fine, G. A. (1987) *With the Boys* (Chicago: University of Chicago Press).

Finkelhor, D. (1979) *Sexually Victimised Children* (New York: Free Press).

Garofalo, J. (1979) 'Victimisation and the fear of crime' *Journal of Research in Crime and Delinquency*, vol. 16, pp. 80–97.

Gilroy, P. (1987) *There Ain't No Black in the Union Jack* (London: Hutchinson Educational: Unwin Hyman).

Gordon, M. and Riger, S. (1988) *The Female Fear* (New York: Free Press).

Gottfredson, M. (1984) *Victims of Crime: the Dimensions of Risk*

(London: HMSO).
Grade, M. (1989) *Report of the Working Group on the Fear of Crime* (London: HOCPU).
Groth, A. N. and Gary, T. (1982) 'Heterosexuality, homosexuality, and pedophilia: sexual offences against children and adult sexual orientation', in A. Sacco (ed.) *Male Rape* (New York: AMS Press).
Herrnstein, R. J. and Wilson, J. Q. (1985) *Crime and Human Nature* (New York: Simon & Schuster).
Hill, G., Howell, F. and Driver, E. (1985) 'Gender, fear and protective handgun ownership', *Criminology*, vol. 23, no. 3, pp. 541–52.
Hindelang, M., Gottfredson, M. and Garofalo, J. (1978) *The Victims of Personal Crime* (Cambridge, MA: Ballinger).
Holland, J., Ramazanolu, C., and Scott, S. (1990) 'Managing risk and experiencing danger: tensions between government AIDS educational policy and young women's sexuality', *Gender and Education*, July.
Hough, M. and Mayhew, P. (1983) *The British Crime Survey* (London: HMSO).
Hough, M. and Mayhew, P. (1985) *Taking Account of Crime* (London: HMSO).
Jones, T., MacLean, B. and Young, J. (1986) *The Islington Crime Survey* (London: Gower).
Kelly, L. (1988) *Surviving Sexual Violence* (Oxford: Polity).
Kennedy, L. W. and Silverman, R. A. (1985) 'Perceptions of social diversity and fear of crime', *Environment and Behaviour*, vol. 17, pp. 275–97.
Lavrakas, P. and Lewis D. (1980) 'Conceptualisation and measurement of citizens: crime prevention behaviours', *Journal of Research in Crime and Delinquency*, vol. 17, pp. 254–73.
Lea, J. and Young, J. (1984) *What's to Be Done about Law and Order?* (London: Penguin).
Lewis, D. and Maxfield, M. (1980) 'Fear in the neighbourhoods: an investigation of the impact of crime', *Journal of Research in Crime and Delinquency*, vol. 17, pp. 160–89.
Lewis, D. and Salem, G. (1986) *Fear of Crime: Incivility and the Production of a Social Problem* (Oxford: Transaction).
Lockwood, D. (1980) *Prison Sexual Violence* (New York: Elsevier).
Market Intelligence (1990) 'Home security' report.
Maxfield, M. (1984) *Fear of Crime in England and Wales* (London: HMSO).

BIBLIOGRAPHY

Maxfield, M. (1988) *Explaining Fear of Crime: Evidence from the 1984 British Crime Survey* (London: HORU).

Mayhew, P. (1986) 'The effects of crime: victims, the public and fear' in *Research on Victimisation*, Collected Studies in Criminological Research, vol. XXIII (Strasbourg: Council of Europe), pp. 67–103.

Mayhew, P., Dowds, L. and Elliot, D. (1989) *The 1988 British Crime Survey* (London: HMSO).

Mayhew, P., N. A. Maung and C. Mirrlees-Black (1992) *The 1992 British Crime Survey* (London: HMSO).

Merry, S. E. (1981) *Urban Danger: Life in a Neighbourhood of Stranger* (Philadelphia, PA: Temple University Press).

Middlesex Polytechnic (1990) *The Second Islington Crime Survey*.

Miller, E. (1986) *Street Women* (Philadelphia, PA: Temple University Press).

Pate, T., Skogan, W. and Sherman, L. (1985) *Fear of Crime and Policing* (Washington DC: Police Foundation).

Pearson, G. (1983) *Hooligan: A History of Respectable Fears* (London: Macmillan).

Research & Forecasts, Inc. with Friedberg, A. (1983) *America Afraid: How Fear of Crime Changes the Way We Live* (New York: New American Library).

Russell, D. E. H. (1973) *The Politics of Rape* (New York: Free Press).

Russell, D. E. H. (1982) *Rape in Marriage* (New York: Macmillan).

Ryan, T. (1985) 'Roots of masculinity', in A. Metcalf and M. Humphries, *The Sexuality of Men* (London: Pluto), pp. 15–27.

Seidler, V. (1980) 'Raging Bull', *Achilles Heel*, no. 5.

Skogan, W. and Maxfield, M. (1981) *Coping with Crime* (London: Sage).

Smith, L. J. F. (1989) *Concerns About Rape* (London: HMSO).

Smith, S. (1984) 'Negotiating ethnicity in an uncertain environment', *Ethnic and Racial Studies*, vol. 7, no. 3, pp. 360–73.

Smith, S. (1986) *Crime, Space and Society* (Cambridge: Cambridge University Press).

Stanko, E. A. (1988) 'Fear of crime and the myth of the safe home: a feminist critique of criminology', in K. Yllo and M. Bograd (eds), *Feminist Perspectives on Wife Abuse* (London: Sage).

Stanko, E. A. (1985) *Intimate Intrusions: Women's Experience of Male Violence* (London: Unwin Hyman).

Tyler, T. (1980) 'Impact of directly and indirectly experienced events: the origin of crime-related judgements and behaviours', *Journal of Personality and Social Psychology*, vol. 39, no. 1, pp. 3–28.

US Department of Justice (1988) *Report to the Nation on Crime and*

Justice (Washington DC: US Printing Office).
Warshaw, R. (1989) *I Never Called It Rape* (New York: Harper & Row).
Wilson, J. and Kelling, G. 'Broken windows', *Atlantic Monthly*, vol. 249, p. 29–38.
Wooden, W. S. and Parker, J. (1982) *Men Behind Bars: Sexual Exploitation in Prison* (New York: Da Capo Press).

INDEX

battering, 6; see physical assault
Bennett, Trevor, 159
British Crime Survey, 30, 122
bullying, 60–2, 89, 112
Burgess, A., 156

Chambers, G., 157
coercive sexuality, 91–4
Cohen, L., 155
Conklin, J., 159
Counsell, Gail, 41
crime surveys, 5–6, 9, 20–1, 30, 42, 76, 109, 122
Currie, E., 158

danger: image of, 2, 7, 9, 34–5, 41, 43, 45, 50; risk of, 3, 5, 17, 67–8, 80; at work, 24–8; at home, 28–32; and street life, 42–5, 107–8
Devor, H., 159
Dowds, L., 156, 157
Driver, E., 156

Edwards, S., 157
Elliot, D., 156, 157

fear of crime, 4–5, 145–7; and social privilege, 6; image of, 7
fear reduction experiments, 147
Felson, M., 155
Fine, Gary Alan, 113, 115, 158
Finkelhor, David, 114, 158

Garofalo, J., 155, 157, 159
Gary, T., 158
Gilroy, P., 158
Gordon, Margaret, 101, 121, 157, 158, 159
Gottfredson, M., 155, 157, 159
Grade, M., 159
Groth, N., 158

Herrnstein, R.J., 158
Hill, G., 156
Hindelang, M., 155, 157, 159

Holland, J., 157
Holmstrom, L., 156
Home Office, 86
home security industry, 28–9, 39, 150–1
homosexuals: violence against, 8, 112–14, 135–43; hostility towards, 113
Hough, M., 156, 157, 158
Howell, F., 157

indecent exposure, 41

Joeman, L., 157
Jones, T., 160

Kelling, George, 147, 159
Kelly, Liz, 56, 139, 155, 156, 157, 158
Kennedy, L. W., 159

Lady Smith, 12
Lamplugh, Suzy, 26
Lavrakas, P., 159
Lea, J., 158
Lewis, D., 159
Lockwood, D., 158

MacLean, B., 160
masculinity: 'real man', 110–12, 129; as vulnerability, 11, 110, 129; as hierarchy, 115
Maxfield, M., 157, 158, 159
Mayhew, P., 156, 157, 158
men: as victims of crime, 5, 109; and violence, 9, 75–6, 118–21; as interviewed subjects, 11; as victims of sexual abuse, 114; and fair fights, 116; and risk taking, 117; and safety; 122; and sexual violence, 123–4
Merry, Sally, 132, 158
Miller, Eleanor, 107, 157
Ms magazine, 72

neighbourhood watch, 4, 30, 46
'nothing happened', 78–80, 91–3

obscene phone calls, 98–100, 141

physical assault, 67, 73–8, 105–6, 128; in childhood, 56
Parker, J., 158
Pate, T., 160
Pearson, Geoffrey, 145, 159
Phillips, C., 157
police: and fear of crime, 4, 9, 48–50, 147; as agents of violence, 136
precautionary strategies, for safety, 5–8, 13–16, 47
prison, and sexual violence, 123–4

racial violence, 62–5, 114–15, 132–5, 140
rape, 33, 47, 49–50, 68–72, 94, 104–5; in prison, 123–4

INDEX

Ramazanolu, C., 157
reform schools, violence in, 63, 114, 120
Research & Forecasts, Inc., 156
Riger, Stephanie, 101, 121, 157, 158, 159
Russell, Diana, 72, 88, 155, 156, 157
Ryan, Tom, 111, 158

safekeeping, 52–3
safety, image of, 35–8
safety advice, 1–3, 48–9, 86–8
Salem, G., 159
Scott, S., 157
Seidler, Vic, 110, 115, 158
sexual abuse, in childhood, 7, 54–9, 88–9
sexual danger, 7; and power, 8
sexual harassment: on street, 95–7; at work, 25, 97; from authorities, 97–8; from friends, 98; as sport, 113
Shatner, William, 2
Sherman, L., 160
Silverman, R. A., 159
Skogan, W., 157, 159, 160
Smith, L. J. F., 155
Smith, Susan, 131, 158, 159
Stanko, E. A., 155
Stockdale, J., 157
Stuart, Carol, 1–2
Stuart, Charles, 1–2

Tombs, J., 158

Tyler, T., 159

US Department of Justice, 156

victimisation, long term effects, 52, 67, 70–2, 75, 104
Victimisation Risk Survey, 30
violence: life threatening, and safety, 33, 68–78; random, 2, 48, 100–1; as 'ordinary', 5

Warshaw, R., 155, 156
weapons, and safety, 23–4, 42–3
Wilson, James, 147, 158, 159
women: experiences of sexual violence, 9, 11, 72, 88; as conscious of special vulnerability, 18, 85–6, 102–4
Wooden, W. S., 158
Worcester Telegram, 1

Young, Jock, 147, 158, 160